TABLE OF CONTENTS

ARCHAEOLOGY OF EARLY EUROPEAN COLONIAL SETTLEMENT IN THE EMERGING ATLANTIC WORLD

EDITED BY

WILLIAM M. KELSO

SOCIETY FOR
HISTORICAL ARCHAEOLOGY

SPECIAL PUBLICATION SERIES

NO. 8

J. W. JOSEPH, SHA Journal Editor

Library of Congress Control Number 2009942695

Cover Illustration by

Tracey L. Fedor, with permission

J. W. Joseph, Copy Editor

Tracey L. Fedor, Compositor and Designer

New South Associates, Stone Mountain, GA

Society for Historical Archaeology

9707 Key West Avenue, Suite 100

Rockville, MD 20850

Pulished in the United States of America

WILLIAM M. KELSO

J. W. JOSEPH

PREFACE

European exploration and colonization marked the beginning of the modern world. Colonization brought Europeans to new continents and into contact with indigenous peoples. In the wake of colonization, Europeans introduced Africans to the New World and stirred the melting pot. In this new cultural geography, interconnected continents and colonies shared economic, industrial, and physical developments that shaped the creation of creole cultures, formed new nations, and created, for the first time in human history, a world where the events in one part of the globe resonated against the rest.

Historical archaeology is a product of this exploration and colonization. Historical archaeology established a new branch of the archaeological discipline that united the written record with archaeological remains. As a result, historical archaeology is the first global archaeology, allowing comparative analysis of geographically disperse settlements and events of the same period to address cultural processes, behaviors, and adaptations. The papers in this volume illustrate the ways in which historical archaeological research illuminates both the processes and products of European colonization at a number of locations on both sides of the Atlantic.

The articles in this volume evolved out of the Society of Historical Archaeology (SHA) Plenary Session held at the 2007 Annual Conference in Williamsburg, Virginia. The theme of the conference, "Old World, New World, Culture in Transformation," seemed fitting since this conference was the first of a year-long series of events in Virginia commemorating the 400th anniversary of the founding of Jamestown, the first permanent English colony. The articles included discuss, and to some degree compare, the historical archaeology of some of the earliest expansion of Europe along the rim of the Atlantic Ocean and its impact on the native populations. An additional intent of the session was to contribute a broader contextual understanding to the founding story of Jamestown by blending documentary and archaeological evidence of the establishment of the early settlements of the Spanish in the Caribbean and the Americas, the English in Ireland and Virginia, the French in Canada, and the Dutch in South Africa. All of these settlements are considered by their authors as well as the processes that have evolved into global modernity. The SHA Plenary session was supported by APVA Preservation Virginia, The Virginia Center for Digital History, and Verizon.

Founded in 1967, the SHA is dedicated to the research, dissemination, interpretation, and preservation of sites from the modern world. The SHA is pleased to present this special publication on the archaeology of early settlement in the emerging Atlantic World.

William R. Kelso, Editor
Historic Jamestown

J. W. Joseph, SHA Journal Editor
New South Associates

WILLIAM M. KELSO

REDISCOVERING JAMESTOWN'S LOST LANDSCAPE

AN ARCHAEOLOGICAL VIEW OF ENGLAND'S EARLY COLONIAL POLICY AT THE DAWNING OF THE ATLANTIC WORLD

ABSTRACT

Archaeological discovery of the 1607 James Fort at Jamestown, Virginia is proving to be a three dimensional window on the evolution of English Colonial policy. In 1606, a group of English merchants and adventurers devised a plan to compete with Spain for the colonization of the Atlantic coast of North America. The following year the Virginia Company sent 105 men and boys to establish a settlement in an area they called Virginia. Their major goal was to plant a secure place from which they could go on to discover the shortest route to the riches of the orient. They also sent men skilled in the techniques required to find and harvest precious metals, gems, and iron ore. Facts and artifacts show that the Company plan for quick profit in trade and industry soon transformed into a cash crop economy.

On 13 May 1607, intent upon implementing the Company "business plan," the English arrived at what would become Jamestown on the James River—that intended wayside camp for exploration west, the permanent port of entry for immigrants, and that place to export riches back to England. In the years that followed, hordes of hopeful English people swarmed to Virginia to make permanent a "Commonwealth" (Barbour 1986 II:225). No one anticipated facing a food shortage, semi-tropical heat, drought, and bad water, together resulting in a horrendous mortality rate among the newcomers. Nor did they have any idea for several years how unrealistic their dreams were of finding gold, silver, and precious stones for the coffers of the Virginia Company. Nonetheless, the settlement survived these disastrous early years to become the first permanent English colony.

The English colonial intent in North America was both similar and different than their European rivals. The search for wealth drove them all. The Spanish had focused their colonial efforts, of course, on taking the Indian gold from Mexico and Peru and sending it back to Spain. The southern part of North America proved devoid of this wealth, despite the tales of its golden cities. Nonetheless, the Spanish persisted in establishing colonies in Florida, as these places would still play a role in the gold business. The settlements' singular purpose was to serve as military/naval bases to protect the Spanish gold fleet from privateers and pirates along the southern North American coast. There was no intent to open a pathway to extensive immigration. St. Augustine, founded in 1565, became the major Spanish base and just inadvertently lived on to become the first permanent European colony in North America.

The year after the English founded Jamestown, France came permanently onto the North American colonial scene with the founding of Quebec. The French, like the Spanish, had a similar motive for a presence in North America. They also needed a place where they could protect their own valuable cargo, furs, for trans-Atlantic shipment to Europe. The exploitation of the valuable furs that were traded along the St. Lawrence River from the American interior gained its required base at Quebec, much to the joy and profit of private sponsoring companies. Like St. Augustine, however, Quebec also only grew into a permanent destination for immigrants, and eventually the capital of New France, by result and not by original design.

Regardless of the original North American colonial aspirations of these three competing European nations, much of the fabric of the three colonial cities has primarily disappeared from their landscapes. Subsequent growth and construction of Quebec and St. Augustine obliterated much of the vestiges of their earliest material colonial past, and changing politics and agriculture masked earliest Jamestown by the 19th century. The interplay of documents and archaeology, however, has dramatically recaptured these three major places that played such significant roles at the dawning of an Atlantic world. Past and recent research at Jamestown is probably the most graphic example.

Records and archaeology leave little doubt that Jamestown was at first a fortified wayside camp and an experimental processing laboratory from which the English hoped they could siphon off the great wealth from the interior and export it to England. Yet the town, partially by design and certainly by evolution, became America's first Ellis Island. In a matter of months the settlement began welcoming England's surplus population and more adventurers who intended to be permanent English Virginia residents. Then, in the space of a decade and a half, settlers rooted themselves on their own land all along the banks of the James River and Chesapeake Bay. These settlements became a chain of family farms that usually produced enough food to keep the farmers alive as well as producing something of cash value to send back home, tobacco. Spain had their gold fleet protected from St. Augustine, and France had Quebec and the fur trade. The scattered Virginia plantations had their golden leaf, tobacco.

What was Jamestown to the Virginia planters? Unlike Quebec and St. Augustine, Jamestown certainly did not serve to protect them from attack. In fact, the wide dispersion of the settlements almost became their undoing.

The Virginia Indians revolted in 1622, killing 347 men, women, and children on the isolated and all but defenseless plantations all along the James. This led to the dissolution of the Virginia Company, but also to the creation of a priceless document that recorded the demographics and indirectly the landscape of the colony and its capital, Jamestown, after its first 17 years.

After the Indian uprising, the English crown took over the colony and ordered a census (Meyer and Dorman 1987:3-71). Taken in 1624, the resulting manuscript lists places, names of occupants, buildings, livestock, weapons, and servants, as well as other things. The population was comprised of 1,284 English men, women, and children, and a handful of Africans. Only 122 of these lived at Jamestown, in 25 houses, while the rest of the colonists were living in the scattered plantations for 60 miles upriver and on the Eastern Shore of the Chesapeake Bay. Consequently, to call Jamestown a town at all was an ambitious misnomer; it was barely a village. It did become, however, the seat of the government after 1619. There presided the governor, council, and 22 elected members of a general assembly representing the dispersed plantations. Jamestown only existed as a well-populated town when the assembly and courts were in session, which brought the people from the far-flung plantations to that central place. This lasted for 92 years until the decision was made to move the government meeting place to Middle Plantation (Williamsburg) in 1699. Thereafter, people begin to desert the town until it reverted to a few taverns and tobacco fields in the 18th century. The visibility of the English cultural landscape of Jamestown, the fortified trading post/immigration point, and even its role as the capital melted away, leaving the only evidence of its former life below ground. Nothing of the original fabric of the town visibly survived to the 20th century except a brick church tower. Ironically, the colonial town that was to be permanent from the start reverted to farmland. St. Augustine and Quebec firmly lived on.

Unlike St. Augustine and Quebec, however, the fact that urban development disappeared over the succeeding years at Jamestown rendered it an ideal, almost Pompeii-like, archaeological time capsule. No urban renewal here. Consequently, for over a century, archaeological study of the almost untouched buried Jamestown has been able to recapture some semblance of what once stood there and some of what was lost to memory. Random and then systematic digging since the late 19th century has indeed recaptured the "lost" place from its life as James Fort through its 92-year history as principal town and capital of Virginia (Cotter 1958:1-166). Recognizing archaeological manifestations of the original and evolving English colony has been among the major results of the excavations.

The first to look below ground for the vanished Jamestown landscape were members or supporters of The Association for the Preservation of Virginia Antiquities (APVA), an organization founded in 1889 to acquire and preserve a commemorative portion of the town site. With the deed to 22 1/2 acres of the island site in hand, and the church tower as a guidepost, some of the founding ladies, an interested engineer, and laborers excavated the site of the church next to the tower and many 17th-century graves (Cotter 1958:219-225). The National Park Service comprehensively uncovered remnants of the newest part of the townscape excavating over 150 structural remains in the mid-20th century. The Park Service also contracted further testing of the same area and a survey of the entire island in the 1990s. Remains of the original fortified town of 1607-1624, thought lost to river erosion, were found by APVA archaeologists beginning in 1994. Excavations of James Fort have been ongoing ever since. This research has been especially revealing of the earliest years when Englishmen, who survived the first shock of the alien Virginia environment, began transforming into Americans. Recapturing this early, lost landscape in surprising detail has been a significant result of this modern applied historical archaeology effort.

In 1993 the APVA committed to plan, support, and administer an archaeological project known as Jamestown Rediscovery on the 22 1/2 acres it owns at Jamestown.

Since then, according to plan, archaeologists have located, uncovered, and interpreted to the visiting public the remains of the original settlement, including James Fort ca. 1607-1624 that, for the past 150 years, most historians believed washed away. Besides locating the lost fort, the excavations also examined the nature and extent of the early settlement and its growth and development. That research has resulted in the recovery of over 1.1 million artifacts, about one-third of which offer new insight into the first years of that English-Virginian colonial experience. As well, the archaeological remains are reflective of an evolving English colonial policy under Virginia Company leadership. The architectural remains, many of the related artifacts, and documentary sources bring into greater focus the process by which English immigrants adapted to the realities of life in Virginia. Archaeological strata show the landscape changing as the colonists became Americans. There are also strong signs that suggest how significant the role of the Virginia Indians was to the English efforts at settlement. The interplay of documents and artifacts leads in an unusually meaningful way to tell this early Jamestown story.

More specifically, 14 years (1994-2006) of excavation and analysis located and interpreted the 1607-1624 James Fort and some of its associated buildings, two wells, trash pits, and burials of original settlers. Later 17th-century structures erected in the fort area were defined, and the ca. 1662-1698 Statehouse Complex was tested and interpreted (Kelso 2006).

The excavations resulted in uncovering the entire perimeter of the fortification, which consisted of three upright log walls (palisades) that once enclosed the one-acre first settlement (Figure 1). Remains of cannon emplacements, known as bulwarks, were found at each of the three corners. The dimensions of the three walls found on the ground essentially matched the specifications reported in a 1610 eyewitness account. That factor was one key, perhaps the most convincing, that most of the 1607 fort remains survived. More evidence was forthcoming.

Figure 1. Aerial view of the site of James Fort with digital reconstruction based on archaeological evidence.

An account of the plan of the interior stated that the fort buildings paralleled each wall with enough distance ("10 yards") from them to leave space for a street on all three sides of the fort. To date, the remains of seven buildings have been found, and they do indeed parallel the walls. Invariably, however, they are 10 feet, not 10 yards, from the wall line, leaving a narrower space for the street all around. Records of a major fire in 1608 described a devastating event—a considerable portion of the palisade and buildings burned. Despite that report, archaeological evidence uncovered so far suggests only one episode of palisade construction and eventual destruction by decay, not fire, all along the wall line. Apparently, at least according to the archaeological record, the reported amount of damage caused by the fire was an exaggeration.

A one-foot-wide trench marked the course of the fort walls. Within two of the ditch lines, dark soil impressions indicated the original position of most of the ultimately decayed upright wall timbers. The third wall-line trench showed clear evidence that the colonists ultimately dug out, purposely removed, and did not replace the posts. Records state that the fort took on a five-sided form, according to

Captain John Smith, in about 1608. If that meant that the enclosure was expanded to the east, then the eastern wall apparently became redundant and eventually removed. Here the historical record and archaeological record of the first fort seem to be at odds. A description of July 1610 leaves little doubt that the wall determined archaeologically, reportedly removed for the five-sided town in 1608, was still standing (Wright 1964:79-81). The "ground truth" is strong; the confusion obviously lies in misinterpretation caused by the meaning of the words. Probably the "town" became five-sided while the fort within it stayed triangular until 1610 when the third "redundant" wall was removed. In any case, this was not the only clue of architectural change over time in the fort.

The archaeological signs of vanished structures and their chronological contexts offer clear evidence that building designs and building techniques evolved through time. Remains of the first fort shelters consisted of crude cellar holes and almost randomly positioned structural postholes paralleling the western fort wall line. These were so close to the palisade that they had to predate the aforementioned creation of the triangular street concept in that area. Early complaints by the settlers that they lived in holes in the ground seem to fit the archaeological evidence in this west section of the town. As crude as these holes were, this area may have been where the members of the council, the president, and the military officers lived at first, under canvas-covered lean-to's attached to the palisade walls. Fill in the cellars produced Chinese porcelain, Venetian glass, a silver 1607-1609 English half-penny, and highly decorative clothing fasteners, suggesting debris left by higher status people. These layers probably did not accumulate there during occupation, however. Suggesting a common analytical problem in archaeology, the artifacts used to fill in an abandoned cellar could have been discarded by anyone living anywhere in the fort. At any rate, tents and lean-to's with crude foxhole-like cellars would make sense for the construction of quick, expedient shelters for the settlers, gentlemen, or laborers during those first summer months of 1607.

There was no evidence of lean-to shelters along the east and south walls. In those areas there were clear signs of more substantial shelters reflecting, it seems, the Company goal of more permanent occupation from the outset. Excavation uncovered remains of what appear to have been long spacious buildings supported by posts set in the ground. Unlike the pit houses on the west, these were sited to honor the 10-foot street setback. They also had more carefully dug cellars at one end. A combination of documentary and archaeological evidence suggests that these large buildings, probably barracks and/or quarters for groups of soldiers, laborers, and even the younger gentlemen, were lightly framed but amply covered with clay and roofed with thatch. The first carpenter sent to the colony, John Laxon, was from Lincolnshire where these "mud-and-stud" building techniques were common. Many have survived there for centuries, indicating that these James Fort slight-built buildings were more permanent in intent than they appear archaeologically. Such a style only requires slight-built timber and scantling walls that served as the frame against which the thick clay for the walls could be attached. Archaeologically, the wooden frames would leave unevenly spaced, and not necessarily exactly aligned, postholes in the ground when the buildings eventually disappeared. In other words, the thick mud walls

Figure 2.
Experimental mud-and-stud frame built on the site of the James Fort barrack.

can be aligned while the post and stud "skeleton" beneath can be independently crooked and uneven. In any event, it is clear from the nature of these buildings that the colonists were quick to use the building materials they found in their new environment that would fit their English vernacular building tradition. Even the first church was apparently of mud-and-stud construction; it was described as supported by forked poles, or "cratchets," undoubtedly set in holes in the ground (Figure 2).

Again, finding precious metals and gems and other valuable resources that the adventurers thought were likely to exist in Virginia was a major goal for the Company. It is not surprising, therefore, that they sent specialists trained in the processes required to find these things: metallurgists, botanists, iron smelters and blacksmiths, gold refiners, jewelers, and apothecaries. It is also not surprising to find archaeological evidence that clearly indicates that the long-range plans for extractive industries were serious. It is logical to expect to find the sites that were purposely built for the specialists. Two have been found so far—one along the fort street, and one appended to the triangle. The latter structure was also of mud-and-stud construction secured by a palisade extension to the east of the fort. The building remains included a spacious cellar and a room with three brick fireplaces. Recovery of copper jettons, tokens often used by merchants for accounting purposes, found together lying on and imbedded in a prepared clay floor in one room, indicated trading (the jettons) and perhaps brewing (the damp malting process may have been enhanced by the installation of the clay floor) activities once took place there. Inside the fort, along the street setback nearest the north bulwark, a double backfilled cellar of a post-set building was found. Artifacts and industrial waste found tightly sealed in a sequence of floor levels

in the cellars signified varied use of the space over time. Originally, the cellars were the workshop of blacksmiths, then later metallurgists and perhaps pharmacists. Smelting iron and making iron tools were some of the first recorded activities of the Jamestown industrial craftsmen working as early as the fall of 1607. As a final use of the cellar space, workmen carved two ovens into the clay cellar wall. A brick-based flue was added in front of the ovens

**Figure 3.
Post-in-cellar multipurpose service-building site, a subterranean blacksmith shop and experimental lab renovated into a bakery; signs of the early years of experimentation.**

which, along with the absence of any artifacts except a large spatula, leave no doubt that the ovens were used for baking (Figure 3). This last use of the space may date the lifespan of the building. It was located adjacent to the site of the probable governor's house of 1611 and therefore it is likely it served that household. In any case, this specialty building clearly reflects the adventurers' commitment to following the English Company's colonial policy, especially experimentation, adaptation, and permanency.

Excavation also revealed that the earthen cellars in the mud-and-stud houses and shops were artifact-rich deposits.

Figure 4.
Discarded arms and armor from final filling of the multipurpose service building, signs of recycling or wasteful activity?

They contained thousands of artifacts primarily lost during the town's first three struggling years. Like the lean-to pits, however, it was clear that except for a few-inches-thick occupation layer at the bottom, these deposits had been thrown into the cellar holes soon after the buildings were destroyed (Figure 4). Like the fill in the pit shelters, they were merely secondary deposits of domestic refuse; the archaeological significance of their original deposition has been lost. Nonetheless, the quantity and quality of the collection is extraordinary. The cellars contained caches of arms, armor, and ammunition; metallurgical testing equipment; medical instruments; craftsmen's tools; pottery for cooking, serving, and storage; as well as glassware; trade goods; faunal remains; and an extensive collection of Virginia Indian Contact Period pottery, tobacco pipes, stone tools and weapons, and shell beads. The tightly datable objects among them clearly determined a deposition date in the cellar of 1610. Many sherds of the same pots were found to cross-mend from cellar to cellar and to other pits and ditches inside the fort. Clearly, these objects were coming from a common primary deposit source not yet found, or perhaps even findable. The real question, however, is why

these buildings were destroyed and their cellars filled in all at once in 1610. It is likely that the explanation lay in a change in the way the Company would do business in Virginia.

Policy had to change by 1610. Archaeological evidence proves that business had not gone well to that point. The story of the birth years of the colony is a horrific one. In the first four months, more than half of the original settlers died. One account methodically records 25 deaths in just 44 days in the summer of 1607 (Quinn 1967:24-27). The excavations determined where all these men were buried within the fort, adjacent to the west gate. The unmarked fort cemetery contained over 30 individual and double graves. Archaeological tests and positions of the burials indicated that these were indeed the skeletal remains of Europeans (English), and the burials likely dated to the first year (summer) of settlement. Three graves were excavated which resulted in the recovery of the skeletal remains of five individuals—two remains in each of two of the graves and one buried alone. They were all aligned in some way and were found to almost certainly date to 1607 by the fact that they did not disturb any earlier features, the grave fill was devoid of European artifacts, and some had been built over by a 1610 row house complex. The single burial was that of a young teen found with a Virginia Indian projectile point next to his thighbone, probably the cause of death (Figure 5). The arrow wound, however, was not his only health issue. His jaw already had been emaciated from infection, and his collarbone had been broken. The first historically recorded casualty of warfare with the Virginia Indians was the death of a boy, and it may well be that these were his remains. These burials, and particularly the evidence of the suffering boy, speak clearly to the fact that the Virginia venture started poorly. Additionally, near a barracks site, two early-17th-century graves were uncovered: a European man who had died of a gunshot wound, and an elderly woman who had lost almost all of her teeth. Not a pretty picture.

**Figure 5.
Remains of an English boy with diseased jaw, broken collar bone, and an apparent arrow wound to the leg, possibly the first victim of warfare between the English and the Virginia Indians in 1607.**

West of the fort, in a military drill field referred to by the colonists as Smithfield, a single grave of a European man who died in his mid-30s was found. He was laid to rest in a well-built coffin, and a spear-like object had been ceremoniously laid on the coffin lid. This obviously was a man of some prominence. Documentary research determined the spear was a Captain's staff—one indicator that this was very possibly the grave of Captain Bartholomew Gosnold who died on 22 August 1607. He

was the obscure mastermind behind the Jamestown venture and vice admiral of the original fleet.

Over 80 burials were excavated in an unmarked burial ground to the west of the fort, offering a profile of the 1610-1630s Jamestown population. Some of these may be the remains of those who perished during the disastrous winter of 1609-1610 when only about 60 survived out of the population of around 215. The causes of death were reported to range from sickness and disease to bad food, lack of food, bad water, and war with the local Powhatan Indians. Clearly, there was a lack of leadership and diplomacy in the colony. This disarray led to siege warfare by the Powhatan Indians, thereby preventing the colonists from venturing out of their "blockhouse" for food, water, and healthy air (Wright 1964:64).

As stories of the death and suffering came back from the colony, however, the Company began to realize that failure could only be averted and success achieved by sending the true leader of the venture, the governor, to reside in Virginia in 1610. More men, women, money, and supplies came with him. Even before that flotilla, however, the Company had sent a fleet in the preceding year. Three of the ships made it, but not the *Sea Venture* carrying the lieutenant governor, Sir Thomas Gates, and other would-be leaders. A hurricane hit the ship and drove it aground in Bermuda. By the time two ships could be built to bring the castaway officials to Jamestown in the spring of 1610, the situation had turned hopeless at Jamestown. The decision was made to abandon the town.

The Bermuda-built ships then headed downriver carrying the entire Jamestown population off to seek asylum ultimately with the English fishing fleet at the Grand Banks.

The voyage would last only 30 hours. The retreating settlers were intercepted by the incoming Company fleet carrying the true governor, Lord De La Warre, and the realistic resupply of men, women, soldiers, food, and supplies. All reoccupied the empty Jamestown, and one of the first orders of De La Warre was to "cleanse the town" (Haile 1998:466). The archaeological record reveals what "cleansing" meant: the razing of the infested mud-and-stud buildings, and the infilling of their cellars with garbage and trash from a common town "dump." This would seem to explain the landfill of artifacts in these cellars and the remains of the mud walls beneath an apparent sign of devastation. Not so. Rather, the mass destruction of buildings and all the garbage and trash were likely the archaeological signs of an "improving" committed colonial policy. Thereafter a renewed and lasting Virginia colony would emerge.

More signs of this new-found support and adaptation to the reality of Virginia are reflected in the building remains found archaeologically to post-date 1610. These "new" structures were not the slight-built, post-set, impermanent first buildings. Foundations made from local and English ballast cobbles, and brick chimney bases were along the western wall of the fort (Figure 6). The archaeological evidence proves the carpenters, brick makers, and bricklayers were henceforth instructed to build for the long

Figure 6.
Overview of two aligned cobblestone foundations and back-to-back chimney footings found along and inside the west fort wall, likely the remains of two-story timber row houses for the resident governors and other officials after 1610.

term. Gone were the crude post-in-ground type buildings, replaced by these cobble-based structures, which were probably the two story, half timber "faire rows of houses" optimistically and enthusiastically described in ca. 1611. These more permanent, long "row houses" were almost certainly built because of the changing Company policy. Governors residing in Virginia needed a "proper" English house, and so did their councilors and De La Warre's reorganized army.

Other archaeological remains seem to reflect a time of plenty and prosperity after 1610. Two abandoned and backfilled wells were found—one inside and one outside the triangular fort walls. They both dated to the time that the fort stood, but each had been constructed very differently. The earliest one, located near the north bulwark, was lined with split timbers forming a box supported at the corners with upright posts (Figure 7). This appears to have been built like a mineshaft and may have been the work of the gold, silver, and copper miners in the early years. Hundreds of artifacts were found at the bottom due to being accidently lost when the well was in use. After the well was abandoned, the shaft was filled with thousands of discarded animal bones. This seems to reflect the time of prosperity brought about by a transfusion of supplies following the arrival of De La Warre. The deposits were indeed dated after June 1610 by the presence of De La Warre's decorative halberd found at the very bottom of the well.

Surprisingly, a gateway was found facing west to the distant riverbank rather than south to the nearby shoreline, indicating a primary fort orientation toward a landing

Figure 7.
Timber-lined well ca.
1610-1616.

nearest to the river channel. In fact, the island was reportedly chosen for the site of the fort because the channel was so close to shore that the ships could be moored to the trees. In the 17th century the channel only came near the shore on the extreme western end of the island, about 25 acres of which have eroded away. In any event, it made sense to have a main gate facing toward the landing point. This discovery underscores the fact that the 17th-century Jamestown landscape was altered by natural, as well as cultural, forces.

The discoveries of the tangible remains of the fort, its town plan, burials of the colonists, and the exact places where the colonists lived, worked, and interacted with the Virginia Indians have begun to enrich the Jamestown story. The new findings elevate the almost mythological Jamestown tragedy to a more realistic and believable account of trial and error, trial and success. Two examples stand out.

The typical accusation that the bulk of the Jamestown settlers chosen by the policymaking Company were simply "lazy gentlemen"—levied by Captain John Smith himself at the time of settlement, and a whole host of historians ever since—becomes an extreme oversimplification in light of the archaeological evidence. The recent discoveries reveal that at least some of the settlers, perhaps a majority, were hard at work as soon as they landed on Jamestown Island. They quickly secured James Fort on the naturally defendable island. This became the trading outpost from which they could explore the Chesapeake region, just as they were directed to do by the sponsoring Virginia Company. The archaeological remains also indicate that these men gathered commodities and experimented in the manufacture of products that were intended to turn a profit. Additionally, the excavations revealed that the relationship of the Virginia Indians and the settlers must have been more intimate than documents alone have indicated. Artifacts indicating the manufacture of stone tools and weapons in the traditional Virginia Indian manner, and decorative objects such as shell beads, show that the natives were living and working INSIDE the palisade walls (Figure 8). All of these native people were not necessarily adversaries. Some diplomacy must have been part of the settlement scheme.

Figure 8.
Great quantities of contact period Virginia Indian pottery, stone projectile points, knives and evidence of their manufacture, and native shell beads in the process of manufacture found in 1607-1611 historical contexts strongly suggest that a number of the Indians were living and working inside the fort.

Jamestown was the first permanent colony of the English nation. Its establishment ushered England into the Atlantic world of the Spanish and the Portuguese. More importantly, from the precarious English foothold on an island in the Chesapeake Bay region of Virginia grew the global British Empire upon which, it was said, the sun never set. By 1921, the Empire held sway over a population of about 458 million people, approximately one-quarter of the world's population living on about a quarter of Earth's total land area. While British worldwide invasion of the so-called "empty" countries like Virginia was often an unjust and bloody business, the idea of government by the governed imbedded in the Magna Carta came with the conquest. When the imperial colonies ultimately left the fold, beginning with the independence of the 13 American colonies in 1776, the ideas of constitutional rule often stayed on, leaving behind the global legacy of self-government, rule of constitutional law, a free economy, and an international language. Considering political, social, and economic development, these traditions have significantly impacted more than the immediate Atlantic world. Civilization may well be too young for us to know how it will eventually turn out, but the global transplantation of European culture, particularly by the English, one could argue, left legacies that are difficult to minimize in the current global community. The ability of historical archaeology to recapture the "lost" Jamestown landscape helps to lay bare the origins of these Jamestown legacies and the evolving early English approach to entering the Atlantic world.

REFERENCES

William M. Kelso
APVA Preservation Virginia, Historic Jamestowne,
1365 Colonial Parkway
Jamestown, VA 23081-0001

BARBOUR, PHILIP L.

1986   *The Complete Works of Captain John Smith
(1580-1631).* University of North Carolina Press,
Chapel Hill, NC.

COTTER, JOHN L.

1958   *Archeological Excavations at Jamestown
Colonial National Historical Park and
Jamestown National Historic Site, Virginia.*
National Park Service, U.S. Dept. of the Interior.
United States Government Printing Office,
Washington, DC.

HAILE, EDWARD WRIGHT

1998   *Jamestown Narratives: Eyewitness Accounts
of the Virginia Colony, the First Decade, 1607-
1617.* Roundhouse, Champlain, VA.

KELSO, WILLIAM M.

2006   *Jamestown, The Buried Truth.* University of
Virginia Press, Charlottesville, VA.

MEYER, VIRGINIA M., AND JOHN FREDERICK
DORMAN (EDITORS)

1987   *Adventurers of Purse and Person: Virginia,
1607-1624/5,* 3rd edition. Order of First Families
of Virginia, 1607-1624/5, Alexandria, VA.

QUINN, DAVID B.

1967   *George Percy, Observations Gathered Out of
"A Discourse of the Plantation of the Southern
Colony in Virginia by the English, 1606.* The
University Press of Virginia, Charlottesville, VA.

WRIGHT, LOUIS B.

1964   *A Voyage to Virginia in 1609.* The University
Press of Virginia, Charlottesville, VA.

AUDREY J. HORNING

"IRELAND IN THE VIRGINIAN SEA"

A COMPARATIVE ARCHAEOLOGY OF BRITISH EXPANSION

ABSTRACT

English settlements in Ireland and North America were arguably so intimately connected that in the early seventeenth century, Fynes Moryson readily referred to Ireland as "this famous island in the Virginian sea" (Moryson 1907). Yet the oft-cited connections between British expansion in Ireland and in North America mask more complex experiences that are now reflected in divergent historical memories and understandings of colonialism in both lands. Archaeological and historical evidence from 16th and 17th century Ireland is presented to explore the extent to which the English experience in Ireland provides an appropriate model for interpreting New World colonialism.

Introduction - Ireland and America

The year 2007, which marked the 400th anniversary of the settlement of Jamestown (an occurrence popularly linked to the birth of the American nation), also marked the 400th anniversary of an event similarly instrumental in the creation of a state—Northern Ireland. That event was the Flight of the Earls—the departure of the Earls of Tyrone and Tyrconnell and their followers from the shores of Ulster. The flight of the Gaelic leaders of the province paved the way for the Ulster Plantation scheme of James I (VI), aimed to supplant native inhabitants with loyal settlers. Much of the funding for this Ulster Plantation came from the same source as funding for the Virginia Company's colony at Jamestown—from the coffers of the London Companies and individual investors. These English settlements in two very different lands arguably became so intimately connected that the chronicler Fynes Moryson readily referred to Ireland as "this famous Island in the Virginian Sea" (Moryson 1907).

The idea that the Irish plantations of the 16th century served as a testing ground for New World colonialism is common in Atlantic world historiography. In 2005, historian Andrew Hadfield asserted that, "When the Jamestown colony was established in 1607, colonial experience in Ireland formed the only serious precedent and means of making sense of the New World" (Hadfield 2005:174). Material similarities between English settlements in America and in Ireland have been long noted by historical archaeologists. Anthony Garvan was first to explicitly consider the similarities between Ulster Plantation villages and those of New England in his 1951 *Architecture and Townplanning in Colonial Connecticut*, while John Cotter referenced the Ulster settlements in interpreting his pioneering excavations at Jamestown (Garvan 1951; Cotter 1958). In the 1970s, Ivor Noël Hume fuelled interest in the comparative analysis of Ireland and the Chesapeake through his popular archaeological accounts of the short life (1618–1622) of the enclosed settlement of Wolstenholme Towne at Martin's Hundred on Virginia's James River (Hume 1982, 1997; St. George 1990; Hume and Hume 2001). In the 1990s, Charles Hodges and James Deetz interpreted 17th-century fortified settlements along the James River as echoing the bawns of Ireland, while Robert St. George considered the English inspiration for the layout of these bawns (St. George 1990; Deetz 1993; Hodges 1993). More recently, scholars affiliated with the Jamestown Rediscovery program, which has unearthed traces of James Fort on Jamestown Island, have directly linked the fortification and the armaments found within its deposits to the Irish experiences of the Jamestown soldiers (Straube 2006).

Acceptance of the connections between British expansion in North America and Ireland is not limited to American historiography. In summarizing what is known of the archaeology of the Irish province of Munster between 1570 and 1670, maritime archaeologist Colin Breen also refers to the presumed role of Ireland in American colonization: "Ireland then becomes a trial ground for future colonial activity and form [sic] future projects in the Americas and elsewhere" (Breen 2007:190). Irish geographer William Smyth similarly finds parallels between settlement in the two lands: "To English men and women, America was a newly discovered, shadowy and strange land. Yet some parts of Ireland also appeared to them in the same light" (Smyth 2006:436).

Yet these oft-cited connections between British expansion in Ireland and North America mask more complex experiences, which are reflected in very divergent historical memories of early modern British expansion as exemplified by contemporary attitudes towards the 2007 anniversaries (Horning 2006a, 2006b). Before addressing the lessons that might be learned from a consideration of colonial legacies, it is necessary to re-evaluate the extent to which the English experience in Ireland before the plantations of the 17th century provides an appropriate model for interpreting New World colonialism. Given the close relationship of Ireland to the British Isles, it is worth questioning whether colonialism is the most appropriate lens through which to view the role of the British in post-medieval Ireland.

Sixteenth-Century Ireland and the Construction of Difference

English involvement in Irish affairs was commonplace well before the 16th century. In the late 12th century, Irish lord Diarmait Mac Murchada enticed a number of Anglo Norman mercenaries to travel to Ireland from England to assist him in regaining the kingship of Leinster. Their subsequent claims to Irish territory precipitated what has been termed the Anglo Norman conquest of Ireland, which witnessed the arrival of English rule and English settlers, the introduction of a new legal and political framework, the establishment of new manorial-style settlements, and the acceleration of urbanism. The greatest Anglo Norman impacts occurred east of a line stretching roughly from Strangford Lough in the north to Bantry Bay in the southwest. To the west of this arbitrary line, Gaelic clan hierarchies, customs, and social structures remained preeminent, with the Gaelic Irish aloof from English law. While officially subservient to the English monarch, in practice the Gaelic as well as Anglo Irish lords worked within a complex system of semi-autonomous lordships, which owed a greater debt to pre-12th-century Gaelic political structure than to any medieval English model. During the nearly 400-year period between the arrival of the Anglo Normans and the arrival of the forces of the English Reformation, Ireland remained nominally under the control of England. However, the internal political dynamics and regional cultural differences ensured that the island never was unified under any one leader. Each lordship and each urban settlement in Ireland functioned somewhat independently and often in competition with one another. Such competition did not lead to insularity, however. Ireland's ports played a significant role in European trade, while Irish religious houses were affiliated closely and strongly to those on the continent (Nicholls 1972; Ellis 1985; Barry 1993, 2000; O'Keeffe 2000; Duffy et al. 2001) (Figure 1).

From an archaeological perspective, it is not difficult to pin down the material influence of England and the continent throughout medieval Ireland. Extensive, well-established shipping routes connected Ireland with the southwest coast of England, linking ports such as Galway, Cork, and Waterford and precipitating the rise of local merchant elites through the export of Irish commodities. The presence

**Figure 1.
Map of Ireland showing locations
mentioned in the text.**

Ireland increased from a nominal few hundred in the 1530s to 21,000 by 1596 (Canny 2001). Military efforts were accompanied by, and dependent upon, intensified efforts to expose and destabilize Gaelic culture. Unlike the New World and its indigenous inhabitants, 16th-century Ireland was not unknown to the English, nor were the English unknown to the Irish. Yet by the end of the 16th century, this known world became "unknown" through the conscious construction of difference—a process arguably integral to early modern colonialism.

Endeavoring to impose the Reformation upon Ireland, and betraying extreme material anxieties, the English begin to legislate against Irishness. Fearing familiarity and perhaps the loss of a newly constructed English identity, English servitors and soldiers were forbidden from wearing any Irish garb—as were the Irish themselves. The mark of loyalty could be read and proclaimed materially, according to the 1537 Act for the English Order, Habit, and Language:

> *Werefore it be enacted … that no person or persons … shall use or wear any mantles, coat or hood after the Irish fashion … every the said person or persons having or keeping any house or household, shall, to their power, knowledge, and ability, use and keep their house and households, as near as ever they can, according to the English order, condition, and manner* (Henry VIII 1923:112-114).

Such statements imply the existence of an essential and recognizable "English manner"—but this must be viewed as aspirational rather than representational. Sixteenth-century England was hardly a unified country with a fossilized identity. Far from that, it was a land and people undergoing uneven but discomforting transformation—materially marked by the process of enclosure, the rationalization

of continental imports is attested to in the medieval assemblages from urban settlements. The recovery of over 700 sherds of Iberian wares representing at least 87 individual vessels from a series of urban excavations in the port town of Galway, for example, supports the assertion of archaeologist Elizabeth FitzPatrick that "Galway after 1550 was coloured by Spain" (FitzPatrick et al. 2004:364).

This Spanish connection was implicated fundamentally in the fractious character of relations between England and Ireland in the wake of the Reformation. The conquest of Catholic Ireland was increasingly seen by the English as critical in their competition against Catholic Spain—ultimately the same political rationale for English interest in the New World. Underscoring the belief that control would come only through conquest, English forces in of lands, and increasing urbanism. The importance of "improvement" to a new English identity can be read in the 1612 comments of former Irish Attorney General Sir John Davies:

> For, though the Irishry be a nation of great antiquity, and wanted neither wit nor valour ... yet which is strange to be related, they did never build any houses of brick or stone ... plant any gardens or orchards, enclose or improve their lands, live together in settled villages or towns, nor made any provision for posterity; ... being against all common sense and reason.... (Davies 1923:352).

That the language of display and the construction of difference was a weapon was readily understood. According to one English chronicler, "It is to be observed in the proud condition of the Irish, that they disdain to sort themselves in fashion unto us, which in their opinion would more plainly manifest our conquest over them" (E. C. S. 1923:350). The Irish perspective is clear in a 16th-century poem composed by the bard Laoiseach Mac an Bhaird (Davies 1923:292-293), deriding an Irish man for sporting English fashion: "O man who follows English ways, who cut your thick-clustering hair ... Pity that you have not seen your fault, O man who follows English ways" (Mac an Bhaird 1923:351). English writer Barnaby Riche was rather less poetic in expressing his frustration with Irish contempt for English culture:

> the Irish had rather still retain themselves in their sluttishness, their uncleanness, in their rudeness, and in their inhuman loathsomeness, then they would take any example from the English, either of civility, humanity, or any manner of decency (Rich 1609).

More broadly, one can interpret the English anxiety over Irish materiality in terms of the practice of othering inherent in early modern colonial ventures. As a result, reference is found to the derided Irish mantle in later English descriptions of Native Americans and Africans. Both John Smith and William Strachey, well-known chroniclers of the early Jamestown settlement, directly compared the clothing of the local Powhatan tribes with that of the Irish. According to Strachey, the local fashion included "large mantles of divers skins, not much differing from Irish 'falinges' [mantles]," while Smith described the clothing of the paramount Powhatan chief, Wahunsonacaw, as a "fair robe of skins as large as an Irish mantle" (Smith 1910:102,405; Strachey 1953:71; Quinn 1966:24).

Cartographic knowledge was another weapon in the English arsenal, with efforts to gain more credible geographic and cultural knowledge of Gaelic territories intensifying throughout the 16th century. Seventeenth-century plantation maps, in particular, emphasize depictions of the extensive commodities available to planters while symbolically subduing the land (and its people) through surveillance. Like the 16th-century maps of the North Carolina and Chesapeake region drawn by Roanoke governor John White, the land as depicted represents future possibilities, and denies past activity. The plane table as an instrument of war was well understood by those who found themselves captured in a map, as underscored by the oft-cited fate of English cartographer Richard Bartlett:

> our geographers do not forget what entertainment the Irish of Tyrconnell gave to a map-maker ... being appointed ... to draw a true and perfect map of the north parts of Ulster ... when he came into Tyrconnell the inhabitants took off his head, because they would not have the country discovered [emphasis added] (Mahaffy 1912:200).

The territories of Ulster represented the most Gaelic and, from an English perspective, most wild part of Ireland. With the exception of Carrickfergus and Newry, much of the rest of the province remained in Irish or in Scottish control in the 16th century. In the 1550s, English servitor Nicholas Bagenal developed and controlled Newry by carefully balancing his allegiances to the English, Old English,

Gaelic Irish, and Scots. The fortified medieval town of Carrickfergus was strengthened under Captain William Piers, who held the command of the Anglo-Norman castle from the 1550s to 1580 (Figure 2). Like Bagenal, Piers maintained control through careful diplomacy, cultivating the conditional loyalty of the Gaelic O'Neills and the Scottish MacDonnells, while simultaneously denouncing them both in official communiqués to the English government.

The governor of Carrickfergus in the late 1580s was sea captain Christopher Carleill, stepson of Queen Elizabeth's Secretary of State, Frances Walsingham. Carleill had recently returned from the New World before taking up his new post. His New World experiences included accompanying Francis Drake in pillaging and burning the Spanish settlements at San Domingo, Cartagena, and St. Augustine, and stopping at Roanoke on their way back to England to rescue Raleigh's first colonists. Before accompanying Drake, Carleill had already made his name as an adventurer with his 1583 discourse on colonization of the New World. Echoing English attempts to reform the

Irish through their clothing, Carleill was convinced that the peoples of the New World would readily "forsake their barbarous and savage living" and "shall have wonderfull great use of our sayde English Clothes, after they shall come once to knowe the commodite thereof" (Carleill 1927:80-90).

In the 1570s, before Carleill had pondered the sartorial markets of the New World, portions of east Ulster were allocated for plantation by English settlers funded by private investors. The most carefully conceived efforts were those of Sir Thomas Smith and Walter Devereux, the Earl of Essex, in counties Antrim and Down. Designed by Smith, a classical scholar, and employing Roman colonial principles, the colonies were to be organized around nucleated villages linked to towns, based upon cultivation and not Irish pastoralism, and designed to yield profit. Smith, as a plantation theorist, also may have been informed by Spanish colonial practice and its nascent racialization of indigenous populations (Canny 1976:133). Smith's plantation efforts, spearheaded on the ground by his son Thomas, were grossly underfunded and subsequently very

Figure 2.
Carrickfergus Castle, begun as a 12th-century Anglo Norman stronghold, re-edified by the English in the 16th century and used as a British base into the 20th century.
(Photo by author, 2007.)

short-lived. The lands granted to Smith were within the traditional lands of Sir Brian MacPhelim O'Neill, a native leader who had sworn allegiance to Queen Elizabeth and been rewarded with a knighthood. In May of 1572, Smith attempted to defuse conflict with O'Neill in a letter: "Since Her Royal Majesty wishes me to be very close to you in location, I do not want to be unknown to you, hoping that I might become the more dear to you the better known I became.... If you act in a friendly manner, we shall live agreeably and pleasantly" (O'Dowd 2000:162). Such was not to be the case. Forces led by Sir Brian McPhelim O'Neill proactively burned church buildings on Smith's grant— including the dissolved Cistercian house at Greyabbey and monastic holdings in Bangor, Movilla, Newtownards, and Holywood—to prevent their use as English garrisons (Hamilton 1860:485; McErlean et al. 2002:106). The last straw was the murder of Thomas Smith the younger by his Irish servants in Comber in 1573; the plantation was soon abandoned. Any physical gains were destroyed by a combined force of Irish and Scots, proving both the tenuous character of plantation schemes and of the loyalty between Crown and subject.

Violence as Colonial Strategy

Beyond the often hopeless pursuit of profit by a small band of adventurers, perhaps the clearest connection between 16th-century English activities in Ireland and the New World is the centrality of violence. Angered by the role of Sir Brian McPhelim O'Neill in attacking both his and Smith's settlements, Essex seized O'Neill and his family in October 1574. This act occurred while Essex and his company were guests of O'Neill in Belfast Castle, and after they had enjoyed three days of O'Neill's hospitality. While the family was sent to Dublin to be drawn and quartered, Essex and his men slaughtered around 200 of O'Neill's retainers. Six months later, still smarting from the loss of his colonial enterprise, Essex ordered John Norris and Francis Drake to attack the Scottish base on

Rathlin Island, off the north coast of County Antrim. Attack they did, killing all of the inhabitants of the island in an action that violated contemporary military conventions. As described by Essex himself in a missive to the Privy Council, "I received letters from Captain John Norris written from the island of Rathlin which he has taken by my direction and has slain all the people they found there" (O'Dowd 2000:882). Of greater importance to Essex than the loss of life on Rathlin was the acquisition of the island's livestock and crops, which he described as "sufficient to find [support or feed] 200 men for a whole year" (O'Dowd 2000:880-881). Elizabethan Irish forces were notoriously poorly paid and ill-equipped with both munitions and basic necessities, a contributory factor in their brutality towards local inhabitants and a precedent for the force routinely employed against indigenous populations in the Americas. Notable early Jamestown colonists, such as Thomas West, Lord De La Warre, and Governor Thomas Dale, who imposed his draconian Lawes Divine Moral and Martiall on the Jamestown colonists in 1611, honed their skills and attitudes as soldiers for Elizabeth in Ireland.

The career of Ralph Lane, spanning two continents, provides further insight into the Irish and New World experiences of some of Elizabeth's soldiers. Lane, an expert in fortifications, left his estate in County Kerry to govern Raleigh's Roanoke colony in 1585, accompanied by an Irish servant. The failure of the Roanoke colony is at least partly attributable to Lane's violent treatment of the Roanoke Indians, and the murder of their chief, Pemisapan (Wright and Fowler 1968; Quinn 1974, 1985; Kupperman 2007). Following his return from Roanoke with Drake and Carleill, Lane was appointed as Muster Master General for the English forces in Ireland in 1592 and was granted Belfast Castle in 1598. In 1601-1602, Lane re-edified Ringhaddy Castle in County Down, which he described as "a place of good importance to answer the service both by sea and land and fit to curb the rebels bordering upon it" (Mahaffy 1912:319,502) (Figure 3). Lane was a prominent figure in the Nine Years' War, which ended in the defeat of the Irish at Kinsale in 1601, the surrender of Hugh O'Neill in 1603, and the Flight of the Earls in 1607. The oft-cited similarities between the fortified bawns of Ireland and the early wooden forts of the Chesapeake, such as James Fort, Wolstenholmetowne, Flowerdew Hundred, and Harbor View, clearly owe much to the expertise of individuals like Ralph Lane, and the expectations of Elizabeth's soldiery. Those expectations included the predominance of violence over diplomacy, along with the reality that soldiers should not expect to be supported adequately by the Crown.

A similar violation of accepted military practice occurred in 1580, again with a subtext of inadequate provisioning. In 1580, Spanish troops that had come to the aid of the Irish surrendered to the forces of Lord Grey de Wilton at Smerwick Harbour in County Kerry, in expectation of customary mercy. In his own words, however, Grey "put ... in certain bands, who straight fell to execution. There were 600 slain" (Hamilton 1877:lxix). Those certain bands were led by one Walter Raleigh, and are believed to have been witnessed by the poet Edmund Spenser, then Secretary to Grey. As described by William Camden, the decision to

execute, rather than merely capture the Spanish soldiers, was because:

> the English were so destitute of food and clothing that they would have mutinied if they had not been relieved out of the spoil taken from the enemy's fort, and there were no ships to carry the enemy away, this was their conclusion ... that the leaders should be saved and all the rest put to the sword for an example, and that the Irish should be hanged.... (Camden 1923:170).

Culpable for many of the deaths at Smerwick, Walter Raleigh was no stranger to the role of violence, as well as the potential for pecuniary gain in Ireland. Even before Thomas Smith devised plans for his plantation, Raleigh's half brother Humphrey Gilbert penned a treatise advocating English settlement in Ireland. Knighted in 1570 for his military service in Ireland, Gilbert advocated the killing of non-combatants as a terror tactic: "yet did it bringe great

Figure 3.
Ringhaddy Castle, Co. Down.
Remodelled by Ralph Lane.
(Photo by author, 2006.)

terrour to the people when they sawe the heddes of their dedde fathers, brothers, children, kinsfolk and friends, lye on the grounde before their faces" (Quinn 1966:128; Canny 1976:122; Palmer 1993). Gilbert is better known for his 1577 state paper entitled "A Discourse How Her Majesty May Annoy the King of Spain" which advocated piracy. Impressed, Elizabeth granted Gilbert a licence "to discover, take possession of, and govern any lands not already under the rule of a Christian Prince." Gilbert himself was lost at sea in 1583 on his return from claiming Newfoundland, and he never witnessed his half-brother's failed efforts to establish the Roanoke colony.

Carefully constructed propaganda suggested that conquering the native inhabitants of North America would prove far easier than had efforts to conquer the Irish. For example, Richard Hakluyt claimed that "one hundred men will doe more nowe among the naked and unarmed people in Virginiea, then one thousande were able then to doe in Irelande against that armed and warlike nation" (Hakluyt and Taylor 1935; Miller 1998:55). The initial willingness of the Jamestown colonists to develop trade relations must be seen as reflecting not only their own awareness of dependency on the Powhatan tribes, but an instilled if naïve belief in the quiescence of the natives, and native susceptibility to English commodities such as Carleill's cloth. Regardless, violence was always a possibility and, inevitably, an eventuality.

Roanoke and Munster

The Munster Plantation of the 1580s often has been viewed as a blueprint for later New World colonial settlements. The experiences of the Roanoke settlers, however, more directly influenced the Munster Plantation at the level of process as well as persona. More accurately described as the Desmond Plantation, the Munster Plantation was an attempt to reallocate the forfeited lands of Gerald Fitzgerald, the Earl of Desmond. As planned, there were to be nine seigniories of 12,000 acres, each accommodating 91 English planters, and divided into a manor and adjacent freeholds (Morrogh 1986). One of the designers of the Munster Plantation was Attorney General John Popham, whose nephew George (with Raleigh Gilbert, half nephew of Walter Raleigh) would later lead the Plymouth Company's failed settlement in Maine in 1607, excavated under the direction of Jeffrey Brain in 1994 (Brain 1995). The fragmented nature of the Munster Plantation, which consisted of non-contiguous territory in the midst of native-held lands, made a mockery of the idea that planters were starting with an empty landscape ready to be molded into some sort of a reflection of England—a belief as ill-founded as Sir Thomas Smith's expectation that the lands of the Ards were only marginally inhabited and represented "waste" to be cultivated (Canny 1977; Morgan 1985).

Cashing in on his popularity with the Queen, but completely undermining the already problematic plantation scheme, Walter Raleigh acquired a massive grant of 40,000 acres. From his occasional base in Youghal, County Cork, Raleigh directed the exploitation of his lands, encouraging the large scale harvesting of timber from forests in the Blackwater Valley, and arguably exemplifying the commodification of nature that would become the defining element of nascent capitalist ventures in the New World. Raleigh's Irish lands also provided an easier challenge for some of those involved in the Roanoke venture. Scientist and chronicler Thomas Hariot ensconced himself in the recently dissolved Molana Abbey, leased from Raleigh. Former Roanoke governor and artist John White lived out his days on leased Munster Plantation lands near present day Charleville, in County Cork. Edmund Spenser famously entertained Walter Raleigh in Kilcoman Castle, County Cork. Excavations at Kilcoman, led by Eric Klingelhöfer, revealed evidence for rather shoddy Tudor construction, which he interpreted as an expression of overconfidence on the part of the Munster planters (Klingelhöfer 2003:111). The planters saw their efforts, confident or otherwise, almost entirely reversed in October of 1598. Irish forces led by Owny O'Moore, an agent of Hugh O'Neill, the Earl of Tyrone and Gaelic leader of Ulster, damaged and destroyed plantation settlements and structures, including Kilcoman Castle.

Nine Years' War

Comparisons have also been drawn between the guerrilla-style warfare of the Irish kerne and the tactics of Native Americans, as noted already (Straub 2006). Yet more recent analysis of the activities of Hugh O'Neill, the Gaelic chief who led Irish forces against the English in the Nine Years' War, suggests a savvy amalgamation of techniques. Landscape analysis carried out by Paul Logue and James O'Neill at the Yellow Ford, where the English suffered their most humiliating defeat in 1598, demonstrated O'Neill's use of his knowledge of the local environment and topography to trap the superior English forces (O'Neill 2007; Logue and O'Neill 2010). At the same time, O'Neill incorporated up-to-date Continental weapons, tactics, and fortifications to beat the English at their own game. By contrast, English forces, according to Ralph Lane, suffered "extreme peril ... in the late encounter in Ulster for lack of military knowledge" (Hamilton 1890:439). Considering that O'Neill had spent part of his childhood in England and had fought with the Earl of Essex against the Scots, his military acumen should come as no surprise. A savvy, transcultural actor, O'Neill readily traversed the cultural boundaries that historical memory has rendered impermeable.

Faced with the sophisticated tactics and munitions of the Irish, English forces under the command of Charles Blount, Lord Mountjoy, resorted to an extreme scorched-earth campaign that echoed the earlier brutality of Gilbert and Grey in Munster (Figure 4). The firsthand accounts of Fynes Moryson give a hint of the human suffering in the wake of the campaign: "And no spectacle was more frequent in the ditches of towns and especially in wasted countries than to see multitudes of these poor people dead with their mouths all coloured green by eating nettles, docks, and all things

Figure 4.
Mountjoy's scorched earth campaign as illustrated by the destruction of the Irish ecclesiastical center of Armagh depicted by Richard Bartlett. (Courtesy of the Environment and Heritage Service, Northern Ireland. Copy of original held by the National Library of Ireland.)

that they could rend up above ground" (Moryson 1907). The destruction wrought by Mountjoy's forces, and the defeat of O'Neill at Kinsale in 1601, laid the groundwork for the later plantation of Ulster, established in the wake of the flight of O'Neill and his fellow Gaelic leaders in 1607. Despite the ambiguity of Hugh O'Neill's own identity, he has come to symbolize the destruction of a supposedly pristine and traditional Gaelic society by an English colonial power, analogous to the conquest of native New World societies, and memorialized in nationalist memory. But efforts to equate the Gaelic Irish with native peoples of the New World presumes a binary opposition between colonists and the colonized, ignores the long-standing connections between England and Ireland, eliminates cultural complexity in all lands, and also denies the self-aware actions of individuals like the O'Neill.

Archaeology of Gaelic Life

Unfortunately, it must be acknowledged that very little is known about the lives of non-elite Gaelic Irish in the later medieval period, in contrast to the better knowledge of the contact-period native societies of eastern North America. For 16th-century Ireland, we are dealing with regional identities linked to clans, yet regional allegiances may have been ameliorated by the habit of tenants to "vote with their feet," exemplified by the movement of laborers between Gaelic regions and the English Pale (Nicholls 1972). The population of Ireland, in contrast to Britain and much of western Europe, was not expanding and had not recovered from the plagues of the 15th century. Exacerbating this low population density were new diseases brought in by English servitors, who themselves fell prey to what has been described as Ireland's unique "disease environment" (Lennon 2005:9). The sporadic conflict and warfare endemic to Gaelic society also impacted population levels, which then were further decimated as the conflict with the English intensified. Finally, we have to tease out truth from

overstatement in English accounts of Irish "nomadism." Transhumance, or seasonal pastoralism, had long been a feature of rural Irish life. To what extent the practice of moving with cattle between winter and summer pasturage was exaggerated by English chroniclers, or exacerbated by conflict, remains unclear. Those few sites associated with transhumance that have been excavated have yielded chronologically ambiguous deposits, and conceivably could date anywhere from the 13th century to the 18th century (Horning 2004, 2007a).

In considering the plantation settlements themselves, a distinction also has to be made between the "top down" creation of a society as designed by plantation theorists like the ill-fated Thomas Smith, with what actually happened on the ground. What happened on the ground takes us a bit closer to a critical understanding of relations between

Figure 5.
Detail of wicker centering, Dunluce Castle, Co. Antrim.
(Photo by author, 2008.)

natives and newcomers beyond what the plantation theorists intended them to be. Examples include the wicker centering sealed in the fabric of plantation dwellings, as in Randal MacDonnell's Dunluce Castle in north County Antrim (Figure 5) and in Sir John Hume's Tully Castle in County Fermanagh. Material connections between the Irish and English are evident in Ulster Plantation deposits, as at Movanagher, where one of the more notable findings from a 1999 excavation was evidence for a vernacular Irish partially earthfast dwelling exhibiting a subrectangular plan, central open hearth, and swept floor located within the village. Associated artifacts included English border ware and North Devon gravel-tempered utilitarian ceramics alongside hand-built Irish everted rimware (Horning 2001, 2007b). The discovery of an Irish house form and material culture within a plantation village does not necessarily mean that there were Irish living in the village (in contradiction to official regulations). Nor does it mean that the English and Scots settlers were somehow less themselves by association with unfamiliar material culture—but the physical traces do allow for a more substantive discussion of the complexities of everyday life in colonial situations. Similar complexity is reflected in the early deposits of James Fort, which include native ceramics and lithic artifacts in such significant quantities to imply the daily presence of Powhatan people within the fort (Kelso 2006:111-114).

There is also archaeological evidence for discourse and familiarity between English and Irish (and Scots) in war-torn Ulster of the 16th century. Excavation in Carrickfergus under the direction of Ruairí Ó Baoill examined a series of late medieval rubbish pits, which contained a mixture of locally made Irish everted rimware, as well as continental and English imports (Ó Baoill 2007). Although established as an English garrison, the presence of native Irish in the fortified town is clear not only from the material culture, but is also shown in a 1560 map, which depicts circular wattle work Irish houses. Unfortunately, no archaeological trace of these dwellings has been found, but we have no reason to doubt that the poorer local folk were constructing these ephemeral dwellings within the town. Further south, the garrison town of Newry was populated by a mixture of Irish, Old English, and New English, and could never be read as a colonial settlement in the sense of a replacement of natives by transplanted settlers.

Contemporary Considerations

With the exception of a brief, and to some degree unsuccessful, period in the late 16th and early 17th centuries, the development of Ireland does not truly adhere to a colonial model as it would be understood in North America, Africa, or India. Close relations between Ireland and the British Isles, and Ireland and the continent, stretch well back into prehistory. Archaeologists seeking to compare North American colonial sites with plantation-period Ireland must acknowledge the extensive material connections between Ireland, Britain, and the continent, which are archaeologically visible from the Mesolithic period onwards. Even in the 16th century, when the English were self-consciously comparing the natives of the New World with the Irish and trialling ideas of colonial settlement on seized Irish lands, Ireland itself remained intimately engaged in European politics and trade.

At the same time, it also must be acknowledged that ideas of colonialism pervade and structure contemporary Irish identity, north and south. Nationalist thought in the Republic celebrates Independence, force-fitting the complicated relations between post-medieval Britain and Ireland into a colonial model, originating with the Anglo Normans and codified during the plantation period. In the north, emphasis on colonialism only exacerbates the divide between Protestants and Catholics, the former viewed as the heirs of the Planters, and the latter claiming descent from the Gaelic Irish. Assumptions about a colonial past still infuse daily life and linger, perhaps below the surface, in contemporary disinterest in post-medieval sites. In the Republic, the pace of development is bringing the rapid

**Figure 6.
Loyalist paramilitary graffiti (UVF—Ulster Volunteer Force)
on the 17th-century Castle Caulfield. (Photo by author,
2004.)**

because of their place in the broader narrative of American history. Unlike Belfast, in Virginia the word "colonial" is ubiquitous and unquestioned, employed as branding for candles, pancake houses, motels, car dealerships, and subdivisions; a marker assuredly not intended to evoke the violence, uncertainties, and unresolved conflicts of colonial entanglements seemingly so much more evident in a place like Northern Ireland.

In Northern Ireland, the 2007 anniversary of the Flight of the Earls was marked by a year's worth of cross-community discussions, events, and conferences, all intended to encourage reflection and dialogue between the traditions. In Virginia, notwithstanding the events organized by Virginia tribal members and the conscious efforts to address complexity in new museum exhibits on Jamestown Island and at Jamestown Settlement, the Jamestown 2007 anniversary was still popularly promoted as an event worth celebrating. For example, a special January 2007 anniversary edition of the *Virginia Gazette* was packed full of ads extolling the mythic virtues of the early settlers, especially their entrepreneurial spirit. Any consideration of the complicated relations between the early settlers and the native people who initially tolerated and facilitated their existence was absent. While it may be too much to expect that the business community should worry about historical accuracy, advertisements only succeed if there is an audience who understands the message. The core message of the *Virginia Gazette* advertisements could be construed as simple white

destruction of the post-medieval heritage despite the hard work of field archaeologists and organizations such as the Irish Post Medieval Archaeology Group. In the north, some plantation-era sites retain sectarian associations, a factor which inevitably impacts upon their preservation and their public presentation (Figure 6). By contrast, the value of colonial sites in the Chesapeake is implicit

American triumphalism (consider "Jamestown 1607: Our Nation's First Dream for a New Home" MJH Builders; or the more ironic claim of WalMart that "Just like the London Company, we deliver").

Such overt capitalization of complicated and unresolved histories ultimately exemplifies the hollow nature of political gestures such as the "profound regret" expressed in 2006 by the Virginia House of Representatives over slavery and the exploitation of native people, and continues to impede the efforts of Virginia Indians to reclaim their histories and identities. Publicity and public education efforts provided by the Jamestown anniversary origin did provide a vehicle for Indian voices, albeit one that may not have lived up to its promise. A Federal Recognition Act for six Virginia tribes was passed by the House just days before Queen Elizabeth II arrived for the Jamestown anniversary, but now remains stalled in the Senate. As expressed by Monacan Indian Karenne Wood: "Some people are suggesting that they were just making sure that there wouldn't be public protests" to mar the Jamestown commemoration (Wood 2007).

should shift from reliance upon stark colonial models to understandings which recognize the fraught and incomplete character of early modern colonialism. The Irish experiences of the Jamestown settlers were critical to their views of the New World and their treatment of native peoples of the New World. To acknowledge the uncertainties of their experiences and the ever-present specter of violence in their reactions is not to downplay the ultimate significance of the Jamestown settlement, nor to denigrate the settlers' fundamental humanity; rather, it is to acknowledge their humanity on and in their own terms. The post-medieval archaeology of Ireland is important to understanding English colonialism in the New World—its greatest relevance, however, many not necessarily be what it tells us about the past, but how it informs us about the present, and where it may lead us in the future.

Conclusion

Outside of Ireland, many people find it impossible to understand how memories of the events of the 16th and 17th centuries can continue to structure daily life. However, uncritical beliefs about the intentions and actions of early Jamestown settlers and a profound disregard of the role played by Powhatan people remain central to populist memories of American history. The complexity of the rich archaeological record from Jamestown should force a reconsideration of the character of relations between the English and the native peoples of the Chesapeake, as well as of the varied backgrounds and disparate expectations of the settlers. Comparisons between the early colonial archaeology of British North America, and of plantation-era archaeology in Ireland, if they are to be of any value,

REFERENCES

BARRY, TERENCE B.
1993   Late Medieval Ireland: The Debate on Social and Economic Transformation, 1350-1550. In *An Historical Geography of Ireland,* B. J. Graham and L. J Proudfoot, editors, pp. 99-122. Academic Press, London, England.

BARRY, TERENCE B. (EDITOR)
2000   *A History of Settlement in Ireland.* Routledge, London, England.

BRAIN, JEFFREY P.
1995   *Fort St. George: Archaeological Investigation of the 1607-1608 Popham Colony on the Kennebec River in Maine.* Peabody Essex Museum, Salem, MA.

BREEN, COLIN
2007   *An Archaeology of Southwest Ireland, 1570-1670.* Four Courts Press, Dublin, Ireland.

CAMDEN, WILLIAM
1923   Annales rerum Anglicarum et Hibernicarum, regnante Elisabetha, ad Annum Salutis (1589). In *Irish History from Contemporary Sources 1509-1610,* Constantia Maxwell. G. Allen & Unwin, London, England.

CANNY, NICHOLAS P.
1976   *The Elizabethan Conquest of Ireland: A Pattern Established, 1565-76.* Harvester Press, Hassocks, Sussex, England.

1977   Rowland White's 'Discors touching Ireland,' c.1569. *Irish Historical Studies* 24, pp. 439-463.

2001   *Making Ireland British, 1580-1650.* Oxford University Press, Oxford, England.

CARLEILL, CHRISTOPHER
1927   A briefe and summarie discourse upon a voyage intended to the hithermost parts of America, written by Master Christopher Carlile (1583). In *Hakluyt's Voyages,* Vol. 6, Richard Hakluyt and John Masefield. J. M. Dent, London, England.

COTTER, JOHN L.
1958   *Archaeological Excavations at Jamestown Colonial National Historic Park and Jamestown National Historic Site, Virginia.* U.S. Dept. of the Interior, National Park Service, Research Series 4. Washington, DC.

DAVIES, SIR JOHN
1923   A Discovery of the True Causes Why Ireland Was Never Entirely Subdued (1612). Excerpted in *Irish History from Contemporary Sources 1509-1610,* Constantia Maxwell, pp. 351-354. G. Allen & Unwin, London, England.

DEETZ, JAMES
1993   *Flowerdew Hundred: The Archaeology of a Virginia Plantation, 1619-1864.* University Press of Virginia, Charlottesville, VA.

DUFFY, PATRICK J., DAVID EDWARDS, AND ELIZABETH FITZPATRICK (EDITORS)
2001   *Gaelic Ireland, C.1250-C.1650: Land, Lordship, and Settlement.* Four Courts Press for the Group for the Study of Irish Historic Settlement, Dublin, Ireland.

E. C. S.
1923   The Government of Ireland under Sir John Perrot (1626). In *Irish History from Contemporary Sources 1509-1610,* Constantia Maxwell, pp. 350-351. G. Allen & Unwin, London, England.

ELLIS, STEVEN G.

1985   *Tudor Ireland: Crown, Community, and the
        Conflict of Cultures, 1470-1603.* Longman,
        London, England.

FITZPATRICK, ELIZABETH, MADELINE O'BRIEN,
AND PAUL WALSH (EDITORS)

2004   *Archaeological Investigations in Galway City,
        1987-1998.* Wordwell, Bray, Co. Wicklow,
        Ireland.

GARVAN, ANTHONY N. B.

1951   *Architecture and Town Planning in Colonial
        Connecticut.* Yale Historical Publications 6. Yale
        University Press, New Haven, CT.

HADFIELD, ANDREW

2005   Irish Colonies and the Americas. In *Envisioning
        an English Empire: Jamestown and the Making
        of the North Atlantic World,* Robert Appelbaum
        and John Wood Sweet, editors, pp. 172-194.
        University of Pennsylvania Press, Philadelphia,
        PA.

HAKLUYT, RICHARD, AND E. G. R. TAYLOR

1935   Dedication to René Laudonniere's Four Voyages.
        In *The Original Writings and Correspondence
        of the Two Richard Hakluyts.* Works issued by
        the Hakluyt Society, 2nd ser. Hakluyt Society,
        London, England.

HAMILTON, HANS CLAUDE (EDITOR)

1860   *Calendar of State Papers Relating to Ireland,
        1509-1573.* Public Records Office, London,
        England.

1877   *Calendar of State Papers Relating to Ireland,
        1574-1585,* p. lxix. Public Records Office,
        London, England.

1890   Ralph Lane to William Cecil, Lord Burghley,
        December 15, 1595. *Calendar of State Papers
        Relating to Ireland, 1592–1596.* Longman,
        Green, Longman and Roberts, London, England.

HENRY VIII

1923   An Act for the English Order, Habit, and
        Language (1537). In *Irish History from
        Contemporary Sources, 1509-1610,* Constantia
        Maxwell. G. Allen & Unwin, London, England.

HODGES, CHARLES T.

1993   Private Fortifications in Seventeenth-Century
        Virginia: Six Representative Works. In *The
        Archaeology of 17th-Century Virginia,* Theodore
        R. Reinhart and Dennis J. Pogue, editors, pp.
        183-222. Archeological Society of Virginia,
        Richmond, VA.

HORNING, AUDREY

2001   'Dwelling houses in the old Irish Barbarous
        Manner': Archaeological Evidence for Gaelic
        Architecture in an Ulster Plantation Village. In
        *Gaelic Ireland 1300-1650: Land, Lordship, and
        Settlement,* Patrick Duffy, David Edwards, and
        Elizabeth Fitzpatrick, editors, pp. 375-396. Four
        Courts Press, Dublin, Ireland.

2004   Archaeological Explorations of Cultural Identity
        and Rural Economy in the North of Ireland:
        Goodland, Co. Antrim. *International Journal of
        Historical Archaeology* 8(3):199-215.

2006a   Archaeology, Conflict, and Contemporary
        Identity in the North of Ireland: Implications
        for Theory and Practice in Comparative
        Archaeologies of Colonialism. *Archaeological
        Dialogues* 13(2):183-199.

2006b   Archaeology and the Construction of America's Jamestown. *Post-Medieval Archaeology* 40(1):1-27.

2007a   Materiality and Mutable Landscapes: Rethinking Seasonality and Marginality in Rural Ireland. *International Journal of Historical Archaeology* 11(3):358-378.

2007b   On the Banks of the Bann: The Riverine Economy of an Ulster Plantation Village. *Historical Archaeology* 41(3):94-114.

HUME, IVOR NOËL
1982   *Martin's Hundred.* Knopf, New York, NY.

1997   *The Virginia Adventure: Roanoke to James Towne: An Archaeological and Historical Odyssey.* University Press of Virginia, Charlottesville, VA.

HUME, IVOR NOËL, AND AUDREY NOËL HUME
2001   *The Archaeology of Martin's Hundred.* University of Pennsylvania Museum of Archaeology and Anthropology, Philadelphia, PA.

KELSO, WILLIAM M.
2006   *Jamestown, the Buried Truth.* University of Virginia Press, Charlottesville, VA.

KLINGELHÖFER, ERIC
2003   The Architecture of Empire: Elizabethan Country Houses in Ireland. In *Archaeologies of the British: Explorations of Identity in the United Kingdom and Its Colonies, 1600-1945,* Susan Lawrence, editor, pp. 102-118. Routledge, London, England.

KUPPERMAN, KAREN ORDAHL
2007   *Roanoke: The Abandoned Colony.* Rowman & Littlefield, Lanham, MD.

LENNON, COLM
2005   *Sixteenth-Century Ireland: The Incomplete Conquest.* New Gill History of Ireland, 2. Gill & Macmillan, Dublin, Ireland.

LOGUE, PAUL, AND JAMES O'NEILL
2010   The Battle of the Yellow Ford. In *Ireland and Britain in the Atlantic World.* Audrey Horning and Nick Brannon, editors. Irish Post-Medieval Archaeology Group Proceedings 2. Wordwell, Dublin, Ireland.

MAC AN BHAIRD, LAOISEACH
1923   O Man who Follows English Ways. In *Irish History from Contemporary Sources 1509-1610,* Constantia Maxwell. G. Allen & Unwin, London, England.

MAHAFFY, ROBERT PENTLAND (EDITOR)
1912   *Calendar of State Papers Relating to Ireland, 1601-3 (with Addenda) and of the Hanmer Papers Preserved in the Public Record Office.* H.M.S.O., London, England.

MCERLEAN, THOMAS, WES FORSYTHE, AND ROSEMARY MCCONKEY
2002   *Strangford Lough: An Archaeological Survey of the Maritime Cultural Landscape.* Northern Ireland archaeological monographs, 6. Blackstaff Press, Belfast, Northern Ireland.

MILLER, SHANNON
1998   *Invested with Meaning: The Raleigh Circle in the New World.* University of Pennsylvania Press, Phildelphia, PA.

MORGAN, HIRAM
1985   The Colonial Venture of Sir Thomas Smith in Ulster, 1571-1575. *The Historical Journal* 28(2):261-278.

MORROGH, MICHAEL MACCARTHY

1986   *The Munster Plantation: English Migration to Southern Ireland, 1583-1641.* Clarendon Press, Oxford, England.

MORYSON, FYNES

1907   *An Itinerary Containing his Ten Yeeres Travell through the Twelve Dominions of Germany, Bohmerland, Sweitzerland, Netherland, Denmarke, Poland, Italy, Turky, France, England, Scotland & Ireland (1617).* J. MacLehose and Sons, Glasgow, Scotland.

NICHOLLS, K. W.

1972   *Gaelic and Gaelicised Ireland in the Middle Ages.* The Gill History of Ireland, 4. Gill and Macmillan, Dublin, Ireland.

Ó BAOILL, RUAIRÍ

2007   Archaeology of Post-Medieval Carrickfergus and Belfast, 1550-1750. In *The Post-Medieval Archaeology of Ireland, 1550-1850,* Audrey Horning, Ruairí Ó Baoill, Colm Donnelly, and Paul Logue, editors, pp. 91-116. Irish Post-Medieval Archaeology Group Proceedings, 1. Wordwell, Dublin, Ireland.

O'DOWD, MARY (EDITOR)

2000   Thomas Smith Letter to Brian Mac Phelim O'Neill, May 20, 1572, entry 252; Walter Devereux, Earl of Essex to Queen Elizabeth, 31 July 1575, entry 1495; Walter Devereux, Earl of Essex to Privy Council, 31 July 1575, entry 1496. In *Calendar of State Papers, Ireland, Tudor Period, 1571-1575.* Public Record Office, Irish Manuscript Commission, Kew, England.

O'KEEFFE, TADHG

2000   *Medieval Ireland: An Archaeology.* Tempus, Stroud, Gloucestershire, England.

O'NEILL, JAMES

2007   An Introduction to Firearms in Post-Medieval Ireland, 1500-1700. In *The Post-Medieval Archaeology of Ireland, 1550-1850,* Audrey Horning, Ruairí Ó Baoill, Colm Donnelly, and Paul Logue, editors, pp. 467-484. Irish Post-Medieval Archaeology Group Proceedings, 1. Wordwell, Dublin, Ireland.

PALMER, WILLIAM

1993   That 'Insolent Liberty': Honor, Rites of Power, and Persuasion in Sixteenth-Century Ireland. *Renaissance Quarterly* 46(2):308-327.

QUINN, DAVID B.

1966   *The Elizabethans and the Irish.* Folger monographs on Tudor and Stuart civilization. Published for the Folger Shakespeare Library [Washington], by Cornell University Press, Ithaca, NY.

1974   *England and the Discovery of America, 1481-1620, From the Bristol Voyages of the Fifteenth Century to the Pilgrim Settlement at Plymouth: the Exploration, Exploitation, and Trial-and-Error Colonization of North America by the English.* Knopf, New York, NY.

1985   *Set Fair for Roanoke: Voyages and Colonies, 1584-1606.* University of North Carolina Press, Chapel Hill, NC.

RICH, BARNABY

1609   *A short survey of Ireland truely discovering who hath armed that people with disobedience.* Sutton, London, England.

ST. GEORGE, ROBERT BLAIR

1990   Bawns and Beliefs. *Winterthur Portfolio* 25(4):241-287.

SMITH, JOHN
1910   *Travels and Works of Captain John Smith: President of Virginia and Admiral of New England, 1580-1631,* Edward Arber and A. G. Bradley, editors. John Grant, Edinburgh, Scotland.

SMYTH, WILLIAM J.
2006   *Map-Making, Landscapes and Memory: A Geography of Colonial and Early Modern Ireland, C.1530-1750.* Critical Conditions, 16. Cork University Press in association with Field Day, Cork, Ireland.

STRACHEY, WILLIAM
1953   *The Historie of Travell into Virginia Britania (1612),* Louis B. Wright and Virginia Freund, editors. Printed for the Hakluyt Society, London, England.

STRAUBE, BEVERLY A.
2006   'Unfitt for any Moderne Service'? Arms and Armour from James Fort. *Post-Medieval Archaeology* 40(1):33-61.

VIRGINIA GAZETTE
2007   January 2nd Edition. Williamsburg, VA.

WOOD, KARENNE
2007   Frustrated Indians Still without Official Status. *Daily Press* 26 November:B7. Newport News, VA.

WRIGHT, LOUIS B., AND ELAINE W. FOWLER
1968   *English Colonization of North America.* Edward Arnold, London, England.

Audrey J. Horning
School of Archaeology and Ancient History
University of Leicester
University Road, Leicester, LE1 7HR
England

KATHLEEN A. DEAGAN

THE SPANISH ATLANTIC WORLD ON THE EVE OF JAMESTOWN

ABSTRACT

When Jamestown was founded in 1607, Spanish colonial settlements had already been established in America for more than a century. During that time, distinctively American, pluralistic creole social practices and identities had developed and become established in materially evident ways. Although the local expressions of this new American *criollo* society varied widely, they held in common a shared experiential frame of reference based in Catholicism, centralized political administration, class-based social hierarchies, institutionalized race mixture, a mercantilist economy, and the Spanish language. This discussion considers the broad-scale formation of Hispanic American identity as a more or less collective self-awareness of being distant from, and not primarily identified with, the European metropolis. The emphasis is on archaeological insights into expressions of such identity during the first century of settlement (ca. 1500–1600), and principally in the households of culturally pluralistic colonial towns.

Identity and Empire in America

Four hundred years ago, Jamestown was settled at the northern edge of an established Spanish Atlantic World, in which Spaniards, American Indians, and Africans living across vast stretches of the Americas had been engaged with one another for more than a century. Spanish America served the new English colonists as a model (for recovering vast mineral wealth), as a warning (in losing vast numbers of the Native peoples), and as a threat (to perilous early survival in politically contested territory).

Many distinguished historians have considered the myriad intriguing questions related to these American empires (Canny and Pagden 1987; Armitage and Braddick 2000; Taylor 2001; Daniels and Kennedy 2002; Applebaum and Sweet 2005; Elliott 2006). Among these issues are the influences of the Spanish empire on the founding of the English empire, the different ways in which these two Euro-American empires were constructed and then deconstructed, the formation of new frontiers, and the creation of distinct American identities and varieties of regional cultural practices.

These issues also offer fruitful ways for archaeologists to approach the formation of the Atlantic World after 1500, and none of them can be adequately explored in the limits of this article. Nevertheless, an attempt will be made to consider with very broad brushstrokes the Spanish American colonial experience before Jamestown, with full appreciation that the term "Spanish colonial experience" masks the extraordinary variety and diversity of individual and local experience in the Spanish colonial world. That said, however, there did exist a series of general, largely imposed, but nevertheless shared points of reference that cut across local colonial experience. Considering these points offers one kind of framework by which to explore how these understandings were interpreted, negotiated, expressed, and transformed in local settings. It also offers a venue for approaching studies of comparative colonialism in the Americas, a difficult and complex topic for archaeology that is regularly invoked, but, as has been pointed out, rarely achieved (McEwan 2002; Stein 2005), with a few exceptions such as Lightfoot (2005) and Rothschild (2003).

In this discussion, emphasis is placed on the creation of "American" cultural identity, one of the "big" historical issues to which archaeology can both bring original insights and make non-trivial contributions.

Questions of identity are inherently difficult to address in that identity is understood—both as a construct and as a lived expression—as contingent, shifting, and expressed at many different scales of behavior. In keeping with the focus of this essay, considerations of identity are restricted to the very general scale of a more or less collective self-awareness in the Spanish American colonies as being distant from, and not primarily identified with, the European metropolis. Obviously, such awareness developed in different places in different ways and times, and through different historical contingencies; here the emphasis is on life in colonial towns during the first century of colonial occupation. This is not only because of space constraints, but also because the Spanish notions of place, space, and ordered life—*policía*—were firmly and explicitly grounded in towns (MacAlister 1984:134-139; Kagan 2000:26-37). There has been a long tradition in historical archaeology of eliciting expressions of identity by decoding material culture and purposely constructed landscapes, perhaps exemplified by Mark Leone's studies of the Mormon-built environment and William Paca's Maryland garden (Leone 1973, 1984). Dozens of historical archaeologists since the 1980s have focused on the interaction between people, objects, and space as an entrée into identity construction (Wilkie 2000; Beaudry and Mrozowski 2001; Pauls 2006). Likewise, historians working in colonial settings have also tracked emergent colonial identity in the Spanish colonies through such material forms of expression as architecture, urban plans, and portraiture (LaFaye 1976; Kagan 2000; Carrera 2003; Katzew 2004). Anthony Pagden (1987, 1992), for example, examines nativist and nationalist themes in the production of literature, art, chronicle, and architecture. He points out that much of this work celebrated Spanish America's ancestral connections both to American Indian nobility and Spanish nobility, creating a glorious shared past in ways alien to Iberian Spain. Richard Kagen (2000) has tracked differences in the way Spaniards and colonial Spanish-Americans mapped American spaces, showing that sense of space and organization governed Spanish-produced representations of American towns, while their colonial occupants mapped the same towns with a sense of place and community.

Of particular interest is historian Stuart Schwartz's consideration of identity in colonial Brazil, in which he expressed anxiety over the fact that all the sources available to historians were produced by a tiny elite segment of colonial society, creating a bias or imbalance in historical assessments of identity. He commented that "there may be an unwritten history of colonial identity that at present cannot be reconstructed. It is one no less valid than the one we have traced" (Schwartz 1987:16). He was correct of course, and it has been archaeology in the homes and settlements of non-elite colonists that has helped realize his prediction and construct a model of colonial identity formation that could not have been gained through documents alone. Dramatic material distinctions between expressions of Spanish and English colonial "identity" are expressed in these settings.

American Origins

Spain's first American colonizing venture was guided by a template very different from the centralized, bureaucratically complex Spanish American imperium that is more familiar to readers of American history. William Kelso's revealing book on the excavations of the Jamestown fort (Kelso 2006) shows many similarities between that early English colonization effort and La Isabela, Spain's first colony in America. La Isabela was established in Hispaniola by

Christopher Columbus in 1493, and it was not intended to conquer American land. It was rather a Crown-sponsored, public-private trading enterprise modeled along the lines of the Portuguese West African *factorías* (trading enterprises) which, like Jamestown, were intended to trade with American Indians and exploit local resources (Pérez de Tudela Bueso 1983; Stephens Arroyo 1993; Deagan and Cruxent 2002a, 2002b).

La Isabela was under the local administration and control of Columbus who, through a very detailed contract with Ferdinand and Isabela, would share in the profits with the Crown. The 1,500 member Spanish expedition was, as at Jamestown, exclusively male, and many of them—also like those at Jamestown—were fresh from religious wars in Europe. Upon arrival, Columbus wrote that nearly all of the men became sick but that most recovered, and the same happened to the men at Jamestown (although fewer recovered). The men were expected to build and maintain the town, grow crops, and work in the trade operations for a salary. As at Jamestown, the colonists quickly grew disaffected by the hard labor of building a settlement and food shortages, as well as the lack of quick profits.

In 1493, there were no policies for interaction with the Native Americans, other than exhortations from Queen Isabela (similar to those of the Virginia Company to the Jamestown settlers more than a century later) to treat them well and fairly, and to try and convert them to Christianity. Columbus established a pact of alliance with one of the Taíno chiefs, Guacanagarí, in 1492, as Newport did in 1607 with Powhatan. Neither alliance led to peaceful coexistence.

"Starving times" were suffered by settlers at both colonies within two years of their arrival; relief supplies were slow in coming, and, indeed, many died of hunger. Despite the general misery, hunger, sickness, and hardship emphasized in the primary documentary sources for both Jamestown and La Isabela, however, archaeology at both sites has revealed that settlers put considerable effort into recreating the material circumstances and organization of their respective mother countries. Columbus built a substantial walled settlement that reproduced a medieval Spanish Morisco city in architecture, material culture, and spatial organization (that is, an organic non-aligned pattern rather than the more familiar Ibero-American grid plan *traza*). Kelso has shown likewise that Jamestown settlers recreated English housing patterns, industries, and material life to a faithful extent. Had no documents been available for either site, in fact, each might have been thought of as well-supplied and reasonably comfortable in their respective 15th-century Spanish and 17th-century English contexts.

Nevertheless, the private mercantile structures of both of these first colonies ultimately failed. Hispaniola came completely under Crown control in 1502, nine years after the first settlement. There the similarities end. Individual enterprise and mercantile interests continued to develop in the 17th-century Royal Virginia colony, with elected governing bodies, religious pluralism, and an enduring adherence among free settlers to the cultural and material practices of their English homelands (Elliot 2006:134-144). This has been shown many times over by archaeological work at English-American sites dating to the first century of colonial occupation, documenting very English domestic practices, furnishings, food, architecture, and landscape organization (Deetz 1977, 1993; Kelso 1984; South 1977; Honerkamp 1990; Shackel and Little 1994; Zierden and Herman 1999).

Spanish Colonial America

The Spanish Americas followed a very different trajectory. Within 50 years of becoming a Crown colony, Spain claimed most of the Americas south of Jamestown as Catholic, Spanish territory, under direct and centralized Crown control (Figure 1). More than 300 Spanish towns had been formally chartered by 1550, and by 1570 it is estimated that there were some 120,000 Spanish inhabitants, approximately 230,000 black and mixed blood people, and nearly 9 million American Indians (MacAlister 1984:130-

SANTA FE 1610

JAMESTOWN 1607

ST. AUGUSTINE 1565

PUEBLA 1530

VERACRUZ

HAVANA 1515

LA ISABELA 1493

MEXICO CITY 1521

OAXACA 1521

ACAPULCO 1550

SANTO DOMINGO 1502

SAN JUAN DE PUERTO RICO 1521

AGO DE LOS CABALLEROS 1524

CARTAGENA DE INDIAS 1533

NOMBRE DE DIOS 1519

SANTA MARTA 1525

CARACAS 1567

PANAMA 1519

SANTA FE DE BOGOTA 1538

QUITO 1534

TRUJILLO 1535

LIMA/CALLAO 1535

CUZCO 1534

AREQUIPA 1540

LA PAZ 1546

LA PLATA 153

ARICA 1570

POTOSI 1546

ASUNCION 1537

SERENA 1544

VALPARAISO 1536

BUENOS AIRES 1536

CONCEPCION 1550

SANTIAGO 1541

IMPERIAL 1551

VALDIVIA 1552

Figure 1.
Approximate extent of Spanish-claimed territory (shaded areas) and principal towns in the Americas, ca. 1600.

133). Universities had been established in Santo Domingo in 1538, Lima in 1551, and Mexico City by 1553 (Rodríguez Cruz 1973). A printing press was in operation in Mexico in 1539, and Lima established a press in 1583 (Elliot 2006:205). It appears that well before 1600, engagements among Spanish, American Indian, and African people in the Americas, as well as their interactions with the imperial center in Spain, had led to distinctly American, creolized sets of social practices that distinguished the people of Spanish America quite markedly, not only from English colonists in North America, but also from their homelands in Spain, Portugal, and Africa.

From Chile to Florida, and New Mexico to Cuba, life in the Spanish colonies was overseen in almost every aspect by a mutually understood, if essentially ideal, monolithic imperial-religious structure implemented by the Spanish Crown. Catholicism, centralized political administration, life in towns, class-based social hierarchies, institutionalized race mixture, a government-controlled mercantilist economy, and the Spanish language were all found throughout the empire (see Deagan 2003 for the development of this assertion). Although the ways in which these elements were manifested and manipulated in local settings were subject to tremendous variation, they did offer a common frame of reference for social understanding, engagement, and resistance among people in the early Spanish colonies.

One of the most remarkable aspects of the Spanish colonial project in the Americas was, in fact, the ability to impose and maintain a centralized organization across such an extraordinarily diverse and dispersed array of people, environments, and polities. It was undoubtedly in large part owing to the capacity of Spanish imperial structure to accommodate local agency and local challenges that the empire was able to persist. Such flexibility is implied in the widely-cited colonial axiom of "*obedezco pero no cumplo*" (I obey but I do not comply), an acknowledged legal principal in colonial-era Spanish America that was frequently invoked by colonial officials when they wished the Crown to reconsider an edict. Although it is discussed most frequently by historians in reference to colonial corruption, the concept also suggests the delicate balance of power and the possibilities for flexible dialogue between imperial and local interests (MacAlister 1984:204-205; Burkholder and Johnson 1990; Knight 2002:55-62; Elliot 2006:131-133).

Catholicism

Central to the imposition and maintenance of the Spanish American empire was fervent and government-sanctioned Catholicism, and a fundamental intolerance for any other mode of spiritual expression. The justification for colonization itself was explicitly religious, codified in 1493 by the Bulls of Donation issued by Pope Alexander VI (a Spaniard). These assigned Spain "a just title" to American lands, in that they were obligated to evangelize the inhabitants and make them Christians. The Catholic Church—in tight alliance with the Spanish Crown—pervaded nearly every aspect of social life, and it privileged religion as the overriding factor (above race, rank, or gender) in assigning social acceptability. This had a powerful influence on the nature of intercultural engagement among Spaniards, American Natives, and African slaves in the Spanish Americas, and stands in dramatic contrast to the English-American colonial experience.

During the early years of American encounter, Spain energetically engaged in formal inquiry into the nature and capacity of American natives, and struggled, as no Europeans had been required before, to define the degrees of difference and similarity between themselves and the people of the Americas. It was ultimately concluded, and formalized in the 1512 Laws of Burgos, that the American Indians did indeed have souls, were indeed human, and as such would be considered free subjects of the Spanish Crown (Hussey 1932; Hanke 1965; Pagden 1982; MacAlister 1984:153-166; Brading 1991:79). Columbus ignored this at his peril when he tried to enslave Taínos in

1497, inciting Queen Isabella to furiously demand: "What right does my Admiral have to give away my Vassals to anyone?" (De Las Casas 1985:235).

Labor and Social Hierarchy

This position created a fundamental tension between Crown interests in converting and protecting its subjects, and the Spanish colonists' desires to exploit indigenous labor. This was initially resolved by the uniquely American institution of encomienda, under which those Indians associated with a particular allocation of land were obliged to exchange their labor for instruction in Christianity and civilization (although it seems quite clear that the Spanish side of the exchange was largely ignored) (MacAlister 1984:157-166; Elliot 2006:39-41).

In some parts of the Americas invaded by the Spaniards, these obligatory labor regimes figured centrally in the social disintegration and breakdown of traditional cultural patterns among American Indian groups during the first century of contact, particularly in those coastal areas that were among the first to encounter Europeans (the Caribbean, the southeastern United States, and parts of Central America). Archaeological research has shown that in other regions, however, such as Guatemala, parts of the Andes, the southwestern United States, and the interior Florida missions, American Indian social practices were accommodated and left largely unaffected, as long as caciques pledged fealty to Catholicism and the Crown, in addition to serving a useful purpose (for overviews of archaeological work in these regions see Thomas 1989, 1990, 1991; also Weber 1992; Gasco et al. 1997; Palca 1998; Gasco 2005).

The integration of local elites by expanding imperial states is a widespread and possibly essential phenomenon across empires in general (Sinopoli 2001:195-200). Recognition and accommodation of elite Native Americans was a cornerstone of Spanish policy in the Americas, and served in

its own way to mitigate the tensions among Crown, Church, colonists, and natives over Indian labor. By securing the alliance of caciques, it was expected that conversion, labor requirements, and tribute would then be imposed through them to their subjects. This policy generally worked quite effectively for Spanish control in those areas of the Americas with strongly differentiated chiefs and stratified societies (Deagan 1985, 2004; Saunders 1998). During the 16th century, this often was accomplished through marriages between Spanish men and elite or ruling native women. Such marriages represented familiar forms of alliance for both Spaniards and Native Americans, and are well documented throughout Mexico, Central and South America, Florida, and the Caribbean (Morner 1967; Lyon 1976; Burkett 1978; Chipman 1981; Socolow 2000:32-36).

In places experiencing severe loss of indigenous population from disease, warfare, and labor, Native American decline spelled doom for the hundreds of thousands of African people brought unwillingly to the Americas as slaves after 1518. The enslavement of African people was justified by reference to the 1493 Bulls of Donation, the same religious-legal arguments that prohibited the enslavement of Indians. Those Donations, however, implied no obligation to evangelize and convert Africans, since Spain held no territorial presence there. Furthermore, Africa was tainted by the hint of Islamic influence, which was sufficient justification for slavery (Morner 1967; Rout 1976; Landers 1990; Thornton 1992; Landers and Robinson 2006). This was also the beginning in America of the association of blackness and labor, despite the fact that many free black Spaniards had participated in the early expeditions of conquest, and a number of them rose to hidalgo status, gaining grants of land and Indian labor (Landers 2006).

Mestizaje and Marriage

Marriage between Spaniards and Indians had been encouraged, at least officially, from the earliest days of

Figure 2.
Casta paintings attempted to characterize the varieties of mixed-race people in the Americas, essentially for Iberian audiences. These portray, clockwise from upper left, "De Yndia y Cambujo Tente en el Aire" (From Indian and Cambujo [descendant of various combinations of African and Indian], Tente en el Aire); "de Español y Morisca, Alvino" (from Spaniard and Morisca [descendant of a Spaniard and a mulatto], Albino; "De Varsino y India, Canpamulatto" (From Varsino [descendent of a mulatto and Albarazado{descendant of an Indian and a person of mixed black and Indian descent}], and Indian, Canpamulatto); "De Español y Negra, Mulata" (From Spaniard and African, Mulatto). Mexico, late 18th century. Museo de América, Madrid.

Spanish-American colonization. In 1503 Queen Isabela instructed the first royal governor of Hispaniola to see that "some Christians marry some Indian women and some Christian women marry some Indian men, so that both parties can communicate and teach each other, and the Indians become men and women of reason" (Morner 1967:26). While canonical law considered different religions to be an obstacle to marriage, it did not consider race an issue as long as both parties were Catholic. Intermarriage and consensual relationships among Spaniards (mostly men) and non-Europeans (mostly women) accounted for between one quarter and one half of all marriages in some parts of the colonies during the 16th and 17th centuries (Morner 1967; Arranz Marquéz 1991; Socolow 2000:39-41). Marriages between Africans and Spaniards occurred, but were considerably less common than those between Native Americans and Spaniards. Spanish-African and Indian-African concubinage, however, was apparently practiced widely (Morner 1967:30-31; MacAlister 1984:126-127).

The acknowledgment and institutionalization of the resulting mixed racial and cultural categories—embodied in the Mexican *casta* paintings—have been a focus of intense scholarly study (Morner 1967:53-75; García Saíz 1989; Esteva-Fabregát 1995; Carrera 2003; Katzew 2004) (Figure 2). These racial categories not only represented an imperial response to colonial choices and realities, but they also formed a crucial dynamic in defining a peculiarly colonial sense of identity characterized by socio-racial ambiguity and fluidity in a way that was very distinct from that of Spain (Chance 1978:155-159; Boyer 1997).

Mestizaje and Materiality

Colonial distinctiveness and fluidity are expressed powerfully in the materiality of life in Spanish-American households. Archaeological evidence from La Isabela, the first colonial settlement, has revealed that the original colonial idea was one of reproducing Spanish material and cultural practice in America, while excavations at even the earliest subsequent Spanish town sites in Hispaniola showed that this idea was altered quickly (Ewen 1991; Deagan 1996; Deagan and Cruxent 2002b:284-296; Kulstad 2008). Household assemblages in these Spanish towns—regardless of the documentarily established ethnic or racial identification of their owners—consistently reveal that domestic household items (mostly for food preparation) are comprised largely of Native American or newly-created, syncretic European-American-African elements. Hand-built, low-fired, unglazed, locally-made earthenware pots dominate many of these domestic assemblages, in place of the *cazuelas* and *pucheros* found in Spanish kitchens. *Manos* and *metates* (grinding stones), useful for grinding corn, and griddles for toasting corn tortillas and manioc seem quickly to have replaced the Spanish *morteros*, *anafres*, and *sartenes* used for grinding wheat and frying in olive oil (for examples of these Spanish vessel forms see Lister and Lister 1987:100-101).

A similar pattern of pluralistic material incorporation seems also to have emerged in 16th- and 17th-century colonial towns throughout

Figure 3.

Sixteenth-century Cerámica criolla from Puerto Real, Haiti (1503–1578). Similar hand built pottery combining American, African, and European elements is found throughout Latin America. Florida Museum of Natural History.

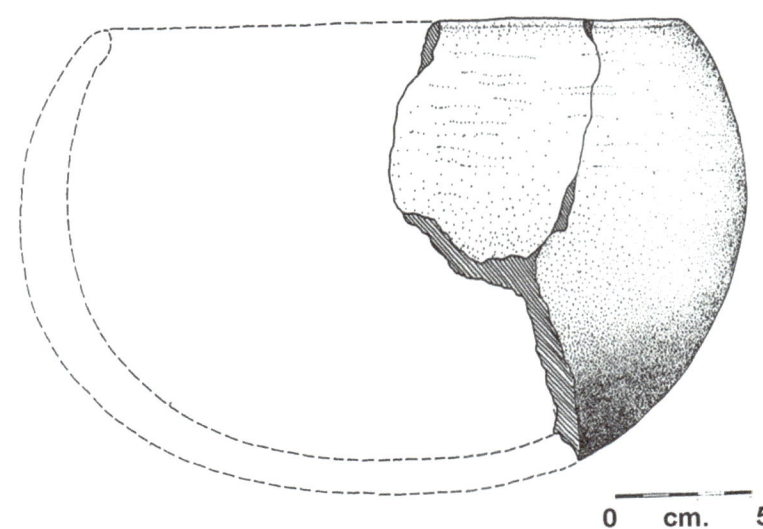

0   cm.   5

Spanish America, presumably wherever American-European-African and racially mixed communities prevailed. This has been documented archaeologically in Hispaniola (Ortega 1980; Smith 1995), Cuba (Domínguez 1980; Romero 1981), Puerto Rico (Rivera and Solís 1993; Solís 1999), Mexico (Rodríguez-Alegría 2005), Argentina (Ximena Senatore 1995), Panama (Linero Baroni 2001), El Salvador (Card 2007), Columbia (Thierren et al. 2002:48-57,78), Venezuela (Vargas et al. 1998), and elsewhere.

Cooking vessels excavated in Spanish-American households in these regions are predominantly (although not exclusively) either local indigenous ceramics wares or locally made "*cerámica criolla*," which is usually low-fired, hand-built pottery incorporating elements of Native American, European, and sometimes African ceramic traditions (this category of pottery is known generally in the early Anglophone colonial regions as "colonoware") (Figure 3). The specific physical attributes of *cerámica criolla* wares vary by region, but whether made by Spanish *criollos*, Africans, Indians, or mixed-race people, these local ceramic traditions share the characteristics of being: (1) formally and technologically distinct from contemporary kitchenware ceramics in Spain, (2) locally produced, (3) exhibiting influence from non-European material traditions, and (4) dominating most kitchen assemblages in "Spanish"-identified households.

This latter characteristic distinguishes *cerámica criolla* from the colonowares documented in Anglophone American sites, particularly in the American South and the Caribbean. Although the colonowares in those regions are locally produced, hand built, and variously influenced by African, American Indian, and European ceramic traditions, they are only rarely found in

Anglo-American households, and they generally occur in plantation slave domestic contexts (Ferguson 1992; Haviser 1999).

At least one category of Mexican pottery combines indigenous elements (decorative methods, motifs, vessel surface treatments, and some forms) with European forms and wheel-throwing production methods (Figure 4). This pottery, known variously as Guadalajara Polychrome, Tonolá ware, or Tonolá Bruñida, is clearly related to late Aztec ceramics, and was incorporated into the Euro-American and Iberian repertoire as a special function ceramic. The strong aroma of its clay when wet encouraged its use by Spaniards for cosmetics and sometimes geophagy (Charlton and Katz 1979; Deagan 1987:44-46; López Cervantes 1990). Although it occurs principally in European-tradition, wheel-thrown forms, it is also a "colonoware" in its integration of indigenous and European practices.

Other items, such as equipment for preparing chocolate, and cups and straws for imbibing South American *mate* tea, have clearly indigenous American origins, both in the commodities and in the methods for preparing them. These preparation items were adopted and produced by Spanish colonists, combining indigenous American forms and functions and European materials and technology (Figure 5).

Figure 4.
Guadalajara Polychrome vessel, St. Augustine, ca. 1700–1750. Florida Museum of Natural History.
Rim diameter: 8 cm.

Figure 5.
Mates (traditional cups and straws for drinking South American mate tea). 18th century Peru. Photograph by A. Taullard (1941).

Euro-American Colonial Production

Spanish-identified colonial households also used items of European or European-tradition origin. By about 1550, however, these were most often the products of colonial, rather than Iberian production. Although these items for the most part continued the technological and stylistic traditions of Iberia, they nevertheless underscore the material difference between colonial and Iberian households (among the few archaeological studies of early modern households in Spain are McEwan 1988, 1992; Amores Carredano y Chisvert Jiménez 1993; and Coll Conesa and Más Belén 1997). By the 1570s, local Euro-American industries and regional trade networks in tableware pottery, glassware, coin minting, jewelry, cloth, leather,

and iron goods were established (Santiago Cruz 1960; Deagan 2002). Glazed tableware pottery, for example—beloved of archaeologists—was after about 1570 typically (although not exclusively) from Mexico or Peru or Panama (Lister and Lister 1987; Rovira 2001; Gavin et al. 2003; Rodríguez-Alegría et al. 2003). Coins were from colonial mints in Mexico, Bogotá, Lima, or Potosí. Glassware was made in Mexico. In other words, the materiality of life in those 16th-century towns demonstrates a clear divergence from household material patterns of Spain, both in the regular incorporation of American Indian and African domestic technology (particularly in, but not restricted to, foodways), and in the early dependence of colonists on American-produced crafts and commodities over those imported from Spain.

Resistance

Another source of material differentiation between Iberian and Spanish-American colonial households of the 16th century was the incorporation and consumption of goods from European nations other than Spain. In an effort to monopolize the products of the American silver and gold mine, Spain's strict mercantilist economic policies mandated that trade in the Spanish American colonies was to be carried out only by Spanish-licensed ships, and only from the ports of Seville or Cádiz (Haring 1964:115-122; Macleod 1984). As both historians and archaeologists have demonstrated, however, this trade was woefully insufficient for providing the everyday needs of the colonists, and by the mid-16th century, colonists in many areas turned to contraband and smuggling to make ends meet (Lyon and Purdy 1982; Skowronek 1992; Deagan 2007).

The Spanish towns of Puerto Real and Bayahá in northern Hispaniola, for example, were forcibly abandoned and burned in the late 16th century by Spanish government officials who found themselves unable to control the enthusiastic engagement of the town citizens in illicit trade with foreign corsairs (Hodges and Lyon 1995). Even such drastic measures were insufficient to prevent contraband trade, and it became a regularized part of colonial economic strategy throughout the Spanish empire. The nature and degree of participation in contraband trade varied widely according to local geography, access to ports, wealth, and social inclination, but it remained a resistant and more or less overt practice until the Bourbon reforms of the later 18th century.

This and other forms of covert and overt resistance to Spanish-imposed regimens by the residents of the American colonies—and particularly the Spanish Crown's accommodation of such resistance—offer another avenue for understanding the formation of Spanish-American identity. From the 15th century onward, the refusal of some local Spaniards, Native Americans, and African slaves to accept imperial mandates altered not only the empire's policies, but also the colonial social order. One centrally important factor in the failure of the initial Spanish colonial effort was the refusal of non-elite expedition members to accommodate the Crown's and Columbus's vision for the *factoría*, with themselves as salaried employees. They demanded land and rights to Indian labor, in rejection of what in 15th-century Spain was considered to be the "natural" social order based on *hidalgueria*. *Hidalgos* (*"hijos de algo"* or "sons of someone") were those who had some claim to nobility, and therefore to freedom from physical labor and taxes. Serfs, servants, and war captives provided labor and were subject to the hidalgos.

In 1497 one of Columbus's former vassals, Francisco de Roldán, living among the Taíno with a group of common-born Spanish compatriots, led a rebellion that forced Columbus to grant land and the labor of those who lived on it to the rebels, regardless of their class. Although this, too, outraged the Crown (and helped lead to Columbus's removal in disgrace), it introduced class disruption and a different kind of social order in Spanish America. It is one of the first instances of the many adjustments made to Spain's imperial colonial project and policy in response to

local and, for the most part, non-elite agency (for discussion of the Roldán rebellion and its implications see Pérez de Tudela Bueso 1955; Moya Pons 1987:19-27; Stephens Arroyo 1993; and Deagan and Cruxent 2002a:201-202).

A great many of the indigenous residents of 16th-century Spanish America continued their resistance to Spanish presence from their first encounters onward, often resulting in Spanish accommodation and policy adjustments (for examples see Weber 1992; Schroeder 1998; Altman 2007). The Spanish imperial government also faced challenges from African and mixed blood peoples, frequently in alliance with American Indians. During the 1520s in Hispaniola, for example, Taíno Indians and escaped African slaves (*cimarrones*) allied to attack Spanish towns. When the Spanish authorities were unable to defeat the rebels, they agreed instead to peace treaties that guaranteed freedom and legitimization of the *cimarrones*. This was a continuing process in the Spanish American world, and similar accommodations were reached with black and Indian rebels in Mexico, Panama, Ecuador, and elsewhere during the 16th century (Thornton 1992; Landers 2006; Landers and Robinson 2006).

Conclusion

By the time Jamestown was established, the structure and dynamic of social life in Spanish colonial America were no longer shaped by an Iberian perspective, or controlled exclusively by a Spanish imperial authority. New kinds of labor exploitation systems, racialization categories, social class distinctions, marriage patterns, economic strategies, and material traditions had emerged through the actions and perspectives of second- and third-generation colonial residents. These included people whose cultural and racial origins lay variously in Europe, America, Africa, or in a combination of these, and who represented a new kind of social and political identity, distinct from either indigenous Europe or indigenous America. Social class was obviously also a critical element, along with racial and cultural origin, in the genesis of Spanish American colonial identity, and it is likely that its emergence was most pronounced among those people who did not share in the wealth of the colonies.

One of the clearest archaeological expressions of this new sensibility was in domestic life, in households, where a new, culturally pluralistic and culturally integrative material world prevailed by the middle of the 16th century. The social mechanisms by which integrative household practice developed were undoubtedly many. It has been suggested that pluralistic commensality in households was a critical factor, engendered regularly by the incorporation of American Indian and African women into "Spanish" households (whether through marriage, servitude, or concubinage). Others have argued that Spanish social strategies for accommodating native elites contributed to such integration, and others point to the organization by Spaniards of native labor and production, or to simple economic necessity as contributing factors (Deagan 1996; DeFrance 2003; Rodríguez-Alegría 2005).

Although most of the comments in this discussion pertain to life in early Spanish American towns, the development of distinctive local identities was probably even more pronounced in rural and frontier regions. There was little social integration of colonized people of these areas into the empire beyond their symbolic acknowledgment of imperial and Catholic dominion, and there is, in fact, considerable archaeological indication that the Spaniards who lived in these communities made far greater adjustments to the American mode of life than vice versa (Weber 1992; Smith 1997; Guitar 1998; Van Buren 1999; Rothschild 2003).

None can speak to the personal visions of individuals about colonial identity, or the values attached to them. But to the extent that material life expresses practice and choice, American Indians, Spanish creoles, and African laborers all contributed visibly to the collective "we" of Spanish colonial households, and in a way that was uniquely New World, and, no doubt, deeply disturbing to the people coming to the new colony of Jamestown.

REFERENCES

ALTMAN, IDA
2007   The Revolt of Enriquillo and the Historiography of Early Spanish America. *The Americas* 63(4):587-614.

AMORES CARREDANO, FERNANDO AND NIEVES CHISVERT JIMÉNEZ
1993   Tipología de la cerámica común bajomedieval y moderna sevillana (s. XV-XVII) I. La loza quebrada de relleno de bóvedas. *SPAL (Revista de Prehistória y Arqueología de la Universidad de Sevilla)* 2:269-325. Seville, Spain.

APPLEBAUM, ROBERT, AND JOHN W. SWEET
2005   *Envisioning an English Empire: Jamestown and the Making of the North Atlantic World.* University of Pennsylvania Press, Philadelphia.

ARMITAGE, DAVID, AND MICHAEL J. BRADDICK (EDITORS)
2000   *The British Atlantic World, 1500-1800.* Palgrave Macmillan, New York, NY.

ARRANZ MARQUÉZ, LUIS
1991   *Repartimientos y encomiendas en la Isla Española (El Repartimiento de Albuquerque de 1514).* Fundación García Arévalo, Santo Domingo, Dominican Republic.

BEAUDRY, MARY, AND STEPHEN MROZOWSKI
2001   Cultural Space and Worker Identity in the Company City: Nineteenth Century Lowell, Massachusetts. In *The Archaeology of Urban Landscapes: Explorations in Slumland,* Alan Mayne and Tim Murray, editors, pp. 118-131. Cambridge University Press, Cambridge, England.

BOYER, RICHARD
1997   Negotiating Calidad: The Everyday Struggle for Status in Mexico. *Historical Archaeology* 31(1):64-73.

BRADING, D. A.
1991   *The First America: The Spanish Monarchy, Creole Patriots, and the Liberal State, 1492-1867.* Cambridge University Press, Cambridge, England.

BURKETT, ELINOR
1978   Indian Women and White Society: The Case of Sixteenth Century Peru. In *Latin American Women,* A. Lavrin, editor, pp. 101-128. Greenwood Press, Westport, CT.

BURKHOLDER, MARK, AND LYMAN JOHNSON
1990   *Colonial Latin America.* Oxford University Press, New York, NY.

CANNY, NICHOLAS AND ANTHONY PAGDEN (EDITORS)
1987   Colonial Identity in the Atlantic World. Princeton University Press, Princeton, NJ.

CARD, JEB
2007   *The Ceramics of Colonial Ciudad Vieja, El Salvador: Culture Contact and Social Change in Mesoamerica.* Doctoral dissertation, Department of Anthropology, Tulane University, New Orleans, LA. University Microfilms International, Ann Arbor, MI.

CARRERA, MAGALI
2003   *Imagining Identity in New Spain: Race Lineage and the Colonial Body in Portraiture and Casta Paintings.* University of Texas Press, Austin.

CHANCE, JOHN K.
1978   *Race and Class in Colonial Oaxaca.* Stanford University Press, Palo Alto, CA.

CHARLTON, THOMAS, AND ROBERTA KATZ
1979   Tonalá Bruñida Ware, Past and Present. *Archaeology* 32(1):45-53.

CHIPMAN, DONALD
1981   *Isabela Moctezuma: Pioneer of Mestizaje.* In *Struggle and Survival in Colonial America,* David Sweet and Gary Nash, editors, pp. 214-227. University of California Press, Berkeley.

COLL CONESA, JAUME AND BIENVENIDO MÁS BELÉN
1997   Cerámica moderna. In *Platería 14: sobre cuatro casas andalusíes y su evolución (siglos X-XIII). Excavaciones arqueológicas ciudad de Murcia, 1,* Pedro Jiménez Castillo, Julio Navarro Palazón, Jaume Coll Conesa, and Jaime Barrachina, editors, pp. 51-64. Ayuntamiento de Murcia, Concejalía de cultura, festejos y turismo, Murcia, Spain.

DANIELS, CHRISTINE, AND MICHAEL V. KENNEDY (EDITORS)
2002   *Negotiated Empires: Centers and Peripheries in the Americas, 1500-1820.* Routledge Press, London, England.

DE LAS CASAS, BARTOLOMÉ
1985   *Historia de las Indias. Vol. 1.* Colección del Commemoración del V Centenario del Descubrimiento de América. Ediciones del Continente, Hollywood, FL.

DEAGAN, KATHLEEN
1985   Spanish-Indian Interaction in Sixteenth-Century Florida and the Caribbean. In *Cultures in Contact: The Impact of European Contacts on Native American Cultural Institutions, A.D. 1000-1800,* William W. Fitzhugh, editor, pp. 281-318. Smithsonian Institution Press, Washington, DC.

1987   *Artifacts of the Spanish Colonies of Florida and the Caribbean: Vol. 1, Ceramics and Glassware.* Smithsonian Institution Press, Washington, DC.

1996   Colonial Transformations: Euro-American Cultural Genesis in the Early Spanish-American Colonies. *Journal of Anthropological Research* 52(2):135-160.

2002   *Artifacts of the Spanish Colonies of Florida and the Caribbean: Vol. 2, Portable, Personal Possessions.* Smithsonian Institution Press, Washington, DC.

2003   Transformation of Empire: The Spanish Colonial Project in America. *Historical Archaeology* 37(4):3-13.

2004   Reconsidering Taíno Social Dynamics after Spanish Conquest: Gender and Class in Culture Contact Studies. *America Antiquity* 69(4):597-626.

2007   Eliciting Contraband through Archaeology: Illicit Trade in Eighteenth-Century St. Augustine. *Historical Archaeology* 41(4):96–114.

DEAGAN, KATHLEEN, AND JOSÉ M. CRUXENT
2002a   *Columbus's Outpost Among the Taínos: Spain and America at La Isabela, 1493-1498.* Yale University Press, New Haven, CT.

2002b   *Archaeology at La Isabela: America's First European Town.* Yale University Press, New Haven, CT.

DEETZ, JAMES

1977   *In Small Things Forgotten: The Archaeology of Early American Life.* Anchor Press/Doubleday. Garden City, NY.

1993   *Flowerdew Hundred: The Archaeology of a Virginia Plantation, 1619-1864.* University Press of Virginia, Charlottesville.

DEFRANCE, SUSAN

2003   Diet and Provisioning in the High Andes: A Spanish Colonial Settlement on the Outskirts of Potosí, Bolivia. *International Journal of Historical Archaeology* 7(2):99-126.

DOMÍNGUEZ, LOURDES

1980   *Cerámica de transculturación del sitio colonial Casa de la Obrapia. Cuba Arqueologica II,* pp. 33-50. Editorial Oriente, Santiago de Cuba, Cuba.

ELLIOTT, JOHN H.

2006   *Empires of the Atlantic World: Britain and Spain in America 1492-1830.* Yale University Press, New Haven, CT.

ESTEVA-FABREGÁT, CLAUDIO

1995   *Mestizaje in Ibero-America,* John Wheat, translator. University of Arizona Press, Tucson, AZ.

EWEN, CHARLES

1991   *From Spaniard to Creole: The Archaeology of Hispanic-American Cultural Formation at Puerto Real, Haiti.* University of Alabama Press, Tuscaloosa, AL.

FERGUSON, LELAND G.

1992   *Uncommon Ground: Archaeology and Early African America, 1650-1800.* Smithsonian Institution Press, Washington, DC.

GARCÍA SAÍZ, MARÍA CONCEPCIÓN

1989   *Las castas Mexicanas: un género pictórico Americano.* Olivetti, Mexico City, Mexico.

GASCO, JANINE

2005   Spanish Colonialism and Processes of Social Change in Mesoamerica. In *The Archaeology of Colonial Encounters: Comparative Perspectives,* Gil Stein, editor, pp. 69-108. School of American Research Press, Santa Fe, NM.

GASCO, JANINE, GREG CHARLES SMITH, AND PATRICIA FOURNIER-GARCÍA (EDITORS)

1997   *Approaches to the Historical Archaeology of Mexico, Central & South America.* Institute of Archaeology, University of California, Los Angeles, CA.

GAVIN, ROBIN, DONNA PIERCE, AND ALFONSO PLEGUEZUELO (EDITORS)

2003   *Céramica y Cultura. The Story of Spanish and Mexican Mayólica.* University of New Mexico Press, Albuquerque, NM.

GUITAR, LYNNE A.

1998   *Cultural Genesis: Relationships among Indians, Africans and Spaniards in Rural Hispaniola, First Half of the Sixteenth Century.* Doctoral dissertation, Department of History, Vanderbilt University. University Microfilms, Ann Arbor, MI.

HANKE, LEWIS

1965   *The Spanish Struggle for Justice in the Conquest of America.* Little, Brown and Co., Boston, MA.

HARING, CLARENCE HENRY

1964   *Trade and Navigation between Spain and the Indies in the Time of the Hapsburgs.* Peter Smith, Gloucester, MA.

HAVISER, JAY B. (EDITOR)

1999   *African Sites Archaeology in the Caribbean.* Markus Weiner, Princeton, NJ.

HODGES, WILLIAM, AND EUGENE LYON

1995   A General History of Puerto Real. In *Puerto Real: The Archaeology of a Sixteenth-Century Town in Hispaniola,* Kathleen Deagan, editor, pp. 83-112. University Press of Florida, Gainesville, FL.

HONERKAMP, NICHOLAS

1990   *Frontier Process in Eighteenth Century Colonial Georgia: An Archaeological Approach.* Doctoral dissertation, Department of Anthropology, University of Florida, Gainesville. University Microfilms, Ann Arbor, MI.

HUSSEY, RAYMOND

1932   Text of the Laws of Burgos Concerning the Treatment of the Indians. *Hispanic American Historical Review* 12:301-326.

KAGAN, RICHARD L.

2000   *Urban Images of the Hispanic World, 1493-1793.* Yale University Press, New Haven, CT.

KATZEW, ILONA

2004   *Casta Painting: Images of Race in Eighteenth-Century Mexico.* Yale University Press, New Haven, CT.

KELSO, WILLIAM M.

1984   *Kingsmill Plantations, 1619-1800: Archaeology of Country Life in Colonial Virginia.* Academic Press, Orlando FL.

2006   *Jamestown, The Buried Truth.* University of Virginia Press, Charlottesville, VA.

KNIGHT, ALAN

2002   *Mexico: The Colonial Era.* Cambridge University Press, Cambridge, England.

KULSTAD, PAULINE

2008   Concepción de la Vega 1495-1564: Lifeways in the Americas' First Boom Town. Master's thesis, Center for Latin American Studies, University of Florida, Gainesville, FL.

LAFAYE, JACQUES

1976   *Quetzacoátl and Guadalupe: The Formation of a Mexican National Consciousness 1531-1813.* University of Chicago Press, Chicago, IL.

LANDERS, JANE G.

1990   African Presence in Early Spanish Colonization of the Caribbean and Southeastern Borderlands. In *Columbian Consequences, Vol. 2, Archaeological and Historical Perspectives on the Spanish Borderlands East,* David H. Thomas, editor, pp. 315-328. Smithsonian Institution Press, Washington, DC.

2006   Cimarrón and Citizen: African Ethnicity, Corporate Identity, and the Evolution of Free Black Towns in the Spanish Circum-Caribbean. In *Slaves, Subjects, and Subversives: Blacks in Colonial Latin America,* Jane G. Landers and Barry Robinson, editors, pp. 111-146. University of New Mexico Press, Albuquerque, NM.

LANDERS, JANE G., AND BARRY M. ROBINSON (EDITORS)

2006   *Slaves, Subjects, and Subversives: Blacks in Colonial Latin America.* University of New Mexico Press, Albuquerque, NM.

LEONE, MARK

1973   Archaeology as the Science of Technology: Mormon Town Plans and Fences. In *Research and*

Theory in Current Archaeology, Charles Redman, editor, pp. 125-150. Wiley and Sons, New York, NY.

1984   Interpreting Ideology in Historical Archaeology: Using the Rules of Perspective in the William Paca Garden in Annapolis, Maryland. In *Ideology, Representation and Power in Prehistory*, C. Tilley and D. Miller, editors, pp. 25-35. Cambridge University Press, Cambridge, England.

LIGHTFOOT, KENT
2005   *Indians, Missionaries, and Merchants: The Legacy of Colonial Encounters on the California Frontier.* University of California Press, Berkeley, CA.

LINERO BARONI, M.
2001   Cerámica criolla: muestra excavada en el pozo de las casas de terrín. *Revista Canto Rodado 1.* Patronato Panama Viejo, Panama.

LISTER, FLORENCE, AND ROBERT LISTER
1987   *Andalucian Ceramics in Spain and New Spain.* University of New Mexico Press, Albuquerque, NM.

LÓPEZ CERVANTES, GONZALO
1990   *Cerámica de Tonolá, Jalisco.* Colección del Museo Regional de Guadalajara. Instituto de Antropología e Historia, Mexico City, Mexico.

LYON, EUGENE
1976   *The Enterprise of Florida: Pedro Menéndez de Avilés and the Spanish conquest of 1565-1568.* University Press of Florida, Gainesville, FL.

LYON, EUGENE, AND BARBARA PURDY
1982   Contraband in Spanish Colonial Ships. *Itinerario, Journal of the Institute of European Expansion* 6(2):101-103.

MACALISTER, LYLE N.
1984   *Spain and Portugal in the New World, 1492-1700.* University of Minnesota Press, Minneapolis, MN.

MACLEOD, MURDO
1984   Spain and America: The Atlantic Trade 1492-1720. In *Colonial Latin America,* Leslie Bethell, editor, pp. 341-388. Cambridge University Press, Cambridge, England.

MCEWAN, BONNIE G.
1988   *An Archaeological Perspective on Sixteenth-Century Spanish Life in the Old World and the Americas.* Doctoral dissertation, Department of Anthropology, University of Florida, Gainesville. University Microfilm International, Ann Arbor, MI.

1992   The Roles of Ceramics in Spain and Spanish America during the Sixteenth Century. *Historical Archaeology* 26(1):92-108.

2002   Preface. *Historical Archaeology* 36(1):1-4.

MORNER, MAGNUS
1967   *Race Mixture in the History of Latin America.* Little, Brown, Boston, MA.

MOYA PONS, FRANK
1987   *Después de Colón: trabajo, sociedad y política en la economía del oro.* Alianza Editorial, Madrid, Spain.

ORTEGA, ELPIDIO
1980   *Introducción a la Loza Común o Alfareria en el Período Colonial de Santo Domingo.* Fundación Ortega Alvarez, Santo Domingo, Dominican Republic.

PAGDEN, ANTHONY

1987   Identity Formation in Spanish America. In *Colonial Identity in the Atlantic World, 1500-1800,* Nicholas Canny and Anthony Pagden, editors, pp. 51-94. Princeton University Press, Princeton, NJ.

1992   Fabricating Identity in Spanish America. *History Today* (42):44-50.

PALCA, JOEL

1998   Lacandón Maya Culture Change and Survival in the Lowland Frontier of the Expanding Guatemalan and Mexican Republics. In *Studies in Culture Contact: Interaction, Culture Change, and Archaeology,* James Cusick, editor, pp. 457-475. Center for Archaeological Investigations, Southern Illinois University Press, Carbondale, IL.

PAULS, ELIZABETH

2006   The Place of Space: Architecture, Landscape, and Social Life. In *Historical Archaeology,* Martin Hall and Stephen Silliman, editors, pp. 65-83. Blackwell Publishing, Malden, MA.

PÉREZ DE TUDELA BUESO, JUAN

1955   La quiebra de la factoría y el nuevo poblamiento de la Española. *Revista de Indias* 60(15):197-252.

1983   *Mirabilis in altis: Estudio crítico sobre el origen y significado del proyecto del descubridor de Cristóbal Colón.* Instituto Gonzalo Fernández de Oviedo, Madrid, Spain.

RIVERA, VIRGINIA, AND CARLOS SOLÍS

1993   La Ceramica Criolla. Paper presented at the 15th International Congress on Caribbean Archaeology, San Juan, Puerto Rico.

RODRÍGUEZ-ALEGRÍA, ENRIQUE

2005   Eating Like an Indian. *Current Anthropology* 46:551-573.

RODRÍGUEZ-ALEGRÍA, ENRIQUE, HECTOR NEFF, AND MICHAEL D. GLASCOCK

2003   Indigenous Ware or Spanish Import? The Case of Indígena Ware and Approaches to Power in Colonial Mexico. *Latin American Antiquity* 14(1):67-81.

RODRÍGUEZ CRUZ, AGUEDA MARÍA

1973   *Historia de las universidades hispanoamericanas: período Hispánico.* Instituto Caro y Cuervo, Bogotá, Columbia.

ROMERO, LEANDRO

1981   Sobre las evidencias arqueológicas de contacto y transculturación en el ámbito Cubano. *Santiago* 44:77-108. Havana, Cuba.

ROTHSCHILD, NAN

2003   *Colonial Encounters in a Native American Landscape: The Spanish and Dutch in North America.* Smithsonian Institution Press, Washington, DC.

ROUT, LESLIE B., JR.

1976   *The African Experience in Spanish America.* Cambridge University Press, Cambridge, England.

ROVIRA, BEATRÍZ

2001   Presencia de mayólicas Panameñas en el mundo colonial: algunas consideraciones acerca de su distribución y cronología. *Latin American Antiquity* 12(3):291-303.

SANTIAGO CRUZ, FRANCISCO

1960   Las artes y los grémios en la Nueva España. Jus, Mexico City, Mexico.

SAUNDERS, REBECCA

1998   Forced Relocation, Power Relations and Culture Contact in the Missions of La Florida. In *Studies in Culture Contact: Interaction, Culture Change, and Archaeology,* James Cusick, editor, pp. 402-429. Center for Archaeological Investigations, Southern Illinois University Press, Carbondale, IL.

SCHROEDER, SUSAN (EDITOR)

1998   *Native Resistance and the Pax Colonial in New Spain.* University of Nebraska Press, Lincoln, NE.

SCHWARTZ, STUART

1987   The Formation of a Colonial Identity in Brazil. In *Colonial Identity in the Atlantic World.* Nicholas Canny and Anthony Pagden, editors, pp.15-50. Princeton University Press, Princeton, NJ.

SENATORE, MARÍA XIMENA

1995   Tecnologías Nativas y Estrátegias de Ocupación Española en la Región del Rio de la Plata. *Historical Archaeology in Latin America* 11. South Carolina Institute for Archaeology and Anthropology, Columbia, SC.

SHACKEL, PAUL, AND BARBARA LITTLE (EDITORS)

1994   *Historical Archaeology of the Chesapeake.* Smithsonian Institution Press, Washington, DC.

SINOPOLI, CARLA

2001   Imperial Integration and Imperial Subjects. *In Empires: Perspectives from Archaeology and History,* Susan Alcock, Terence D'Altroy, Kathleen Morrison, and Carla Sinopoli, editors, pp. 195-200. University of Cambridge Press, Cambridge, England.

SKOWRONEK, RUSSELL K.

1992   Empire and Ceramics: The Changing Role of Illicit Trade in Spanish America. *Historical Archaeology* 26(1):109-118.

SMITH, GREG C.

1995   Indians and Africans at Puerto Real: The Ceramic Evidence. In *Puerto Real: The Archaeology of a Sixteenth-Century Town in Hispaniola,* Kathleen Deagan, editor, pp. 335-374. University Press of Florida, Gainesville, FL.

1997   Hispanic, Andean, and African Influences in the Moquegua Valley of Southern Peru. *Historical Archaeology* 31(1):74–83.

SOCOLOW, SUSAN

2000   *The Women of Colonial Latin America.* Cambridge University Press, Cambridge, England.

SOLÍS, CARLOS

1999   Criollo Pottery from San Juan de Puerto Rico. In *African Sites Archaeology in the Caribbean, Jay* Haviser, editor, pp. 131-142. Markus Weiner Publishers, Princeton, NJ.

SOUTH, STANLEY

1977   *Method and Theory in Historical Archeology.* Academic Press, New York, NY.

STEIN, GIL

2005   Introduction: The Comparative Archaeology of Colonial Encounters. In *The Archaeology of Colonial Encounters,* Gil Stein, editor, pp. 3-32. School of American Research Press, Santa Fe, NM.

STEPHENS ARROYO, ANTHONY

1993   The Inter-Atlantic Paradigm: The Failure of Spanish Medieval Colonization in the Canary and Caribbean Islands. *Comparative Studies in Society and History* 35(3):515-543.

TAULLARD, ALBERTO
1941   *Platería Sudamericana.* Peuser, Buenos Aires.

TAYLOR, ALAN
2001   *American Colonies: The Settling of North America.* Penguin Books, New York, NY.

THIERREN, MONIKA, ELENA UPRIMY, JIMENA LOBO GUERRERO, MARÍA FERNANDA SALAMANCA, FELIPE GAITÁN, AND MARTA FANDIÑO
2002   *Catálago de cerámica colonial y republicana de la Nueva Granada.* Fundación de Investigaciones Arqueológicas Nacionales, Bogota, Columbia.

THOMAS, DAVID H. (EDITOR)
1989   *Columbian Consequences, Vol. 1, Archaeological and Historical Perspectives on the Spanish Borderlands West.* Smithsonian Institution Press, Washington, DC.

1990   *Columbian Consequences, Vol. 2, Archaeological and Historical Perspectives on the Spanish Borderlands East.* Smithsonian Institution Press, Washington, DC.

1991   *Columbian Consequences, Vol. 3, The Spanish Borderlands in Pan-American Perspective.* Smithsonian Institution Press, Washington, DC.

THORNTON, JOHN K.
1992   *Africa and Africans in the Making of the Atlantic World, 1400-1800.* Cambridge University Press, Cambridge, England.

VAN BUREN, MARY
1999   Tarapaya: An Elite Spanish Residence near Colonial Potosi in Comparative Perspective. *Historical Archaeology* 33(2):101–115.

VARGAS, IRAIDA, MARIO SANOJA, GABRIELA ALVARADO, AND MILENE MONTILLA
1998   *Arqueología de Caracas. San Pablo Teatro Municipial,* Vol. 2, pp. 73-79. Biblioteca de la Académia Nacional de História, No. 178. Caracas, Venezuela.

WEBER, DAVID
1992   *The Spanish Frontier in North America.* Yale University Press, New Haven, CT.

WILKIE, LAURIE
2000   Culture Bought: Evidence of Creolization in the Consumer Goods of an Enslaved Bahamian Family. *Historical Archaeology* 34(3):10-26.

ZIERDEN, MARTHA, AND BERNARD HERMAN (EDITORS)
1999   Charleston in the Context of Trans-Atlantic Culture. *Historical Archaeology* 33(3):1-107.

Kathleen Deagan
Florida Museum of Natural History
Box 117800
University of Florida
Gainesville, Florida 32610

MARCEL MOUSSETTE
WILLIAM MOSS

QUEBEC, COLONIAL CITY AND NEW WORLD ATLANTIC PORT

AN ARCHAEOLOGICAL PERSPECTIVE

ABSTRACT

The urban core of Quebec City as a colonial town is approached in the context of the Atlantic world at the onset of Modernity. A theoretical approach to the archaeology of the city is elaborated based on the concepts of landscape and provisioning. This approach is used to prepare a synthesis of physical vestiges unearthed on the principal sites within the urban fabric. This synthesis is constructed on the principal elements of the urban landscape: its topography; the fortifications and port infrastructures; sites for the exercise of power; residences and, finally, industries. The conclusion situates Quebec in the context of New France, particularly by considering it in relation with Montreal.

Introduction

The archaeology of Quebec City during the French regime has, until now, scarcely looked at Quebec as a colonial town. Despite numerous excavations having been carried out, archaeologists have yet to consider this fundamental characteristic—at least to synthesize data—in order to develop a global perspective on the city. Such an endeavor is certainly ambitious—perhaps even premature—but that is what is undertaken in this article in order to draw a general portrait of the city as seen through the material vestiges of its early colonial context. In order to do so, this approach first is defined in the larger context of the onset of Modernity and the creation of an Atlantic world. The question of the permanent establishment of France in the St. Lawrence valley is then addressed. Once these preliminary considerations have been addressed, a theoretical approach will be developed to serve as a basis for the synthesis of archaeological research on Quebec City in relation to its colonial context. This synthesis will be constructed from the principal determining elements of the urban landscape: its topography defined in part by the St. Lawrence River and its affluent, the St. Charles; the fortifications and port infrastructures; the seats of institutional power; private residences and industries. In conclusion, Quebec is examined in the wider context of New France, especially in relation to Montreal, a relay station to the interior of the continent.

Modernity and the Definition of an Atlantic World

During the 16th century, northeastern North America witnessed the beginning of new exploration and merchant adventures—fishing and fur trading—which lead Europeans, particularly the Basques, Bretons, and Normans, to come into contact with an immense continent and its inhabitants, Native American horticulturalists and nomadic hunters. These encounters were not always peaceful, and it was not until the beginning of the following century that Europeans would settle permanently, a prerequisite to the existence of urban centers as they were known in Europe.

These far-off voyages, undertaken during the 16th century by Western Europeans in search of new riches and new territories, are the result of an important structural phenomenon that would leave its mark on following centuries and that historians name Modernity: "Modernity is the first unity of the world, the terrestrial globe caught up in a common adventure, however fragile that community life might be ... a world that tends towards unity" (Braudel 1997:301; authors' translation).

In fact, this rupture with the Middle Ages coincides with the expansion of European capitalism through other continents. According to Immanuel Wallerstein (1984:7), the evolution of this phenomenon occurred in three phases delineated by as many pivotal dates. The phase of interest here is of course the first, running from 1500 to 1650. It constitutes the initial period of capitalism with the creation of a world economy centered on Western Europe with, insofar as this study is concerned, an Atlantic world bridging the heart of this economy and one of its margins, North America (Braudel 1985:86-87).

Historians such as Braudel (1979:287,292) and Fox (1973) have already made the distinction between the maritime margins of France—wealthy from trade and commerce—and the heart of the country—conservative and underdeveloped with its wealth based on landed property. It is this maritime margin of France, adventurous and entrepreneurial, that participated in the development of the northern Atlantic world uniting Europe and the eastern coast of North America. At the end of the 16th century, with knowledge gained through exploration and commercial ventures, France was on the threshold of launching a series of expeditions that would encounter Native peoples of the Great Lakes and the Mississippi Valley and that would result in the founding of a chain of Euro-American outposts that came to constitute a fragile empire.

The French Settle Permanently in the St. Lawrence Valley

When Pont-Gravé and Champlain, who traveled as an observer, came to the Tadoussac trading post in 1603, the situation had greatly changed since the period of Jacques Cartier's voyages 60 years earlier. The St. Lawrence Iroquoians had been dispersed, either as the result of intertribal warfare or diseases imported by Europeans, though it is not yet known why or how. Before being able to penetrate further up the St. Lawrence River, the French had to negotiate an alliance with the Montagnais and their chief, Anadabijou (Trudel 1963:267-268). This was a founding act of great import as it allowed Du Gua de Monts, following unsuccessful efforts at Ste. Croix Island and Port-Royal in Acadia, to establish a trading post in the St. Lawrence Valley at Quebec in 1608 (Avignon 2006).

Over several years, this post came to include several components: the vast fortified *habitation* and the Recollet friars' monastery at the foot of the cliff; the Saint Louis fort and, on the upper plateau, the first farmstead exploited by Louis Hébert and his son-in-law, Guillaume Couillard; and the *Petite-Ferme*, another farmstead 30 miles downriver at Cap Tourmente. These components strengthened the permanence of the post and created the basis for a durable colony that would become the starting point of the permanent French presence on the banks of the St. Lawrence and further into the interior of the continent. Most of the sites associated with this period have been investigated by archaeologists, and the lifestyles of the newcomers, as well as the difficulties they encountered, are now better understood (Niellon and Moussette 1985; Clermont et al. 1992; Guimont 1996; Simoneau 1996, 2008a).

For this period, it is not yet possible to speak of an urban core. Nonetheless, as this would become the city of Quebec, it is possible to rapidly define what is meant by an urban phenomenon and how, in the case of Quebec, this can be understood through an archaeological approach.

An Approach to the Archaeology of Quebec City

For an ecologist such as Odum (1976), an urban ecosystem is first and foremost a sustained system, which is to say a system that cannot exist independently and can only meet its needs for energy input through a parasitical relation with other ecosystems. In the same vein, Fernand Braudel (1967:370) states that "a city only exists as such in light of a lower level of organizations," this "lower level of organization" necessarily being the countryside which must "carry the city" (Braudel 1967:372; authors' translations). In the Middle Ages, the pre-industrial city was enclosed by its ramparts (Hannerz 1980:105-106), and the urban form characterized by these defensive walls becomes so closely associated with the city that Braudel (1967:376; authors' translation) can state that "all cities are worlds apart. It is interesting to note that, from the 15th to the 18th centuries, most if not all cities have ramparts." Fortified walls were a determining criterion for the status of a city.

A city is not, however, only system and form, it is also composed of individuals. Castells (1972:1; authors' translation) indicates that a city is also the "permanent site of dense and relatively large numbers of socially heterogeneous individuals." This text, taken from Louis Wirth, is also quoted by Ulf Hannerz (1980:87-88) who insists on the consequences that the size of the city and the concentration of individuals of different origins and talent have on the creation of an urban environment. Densification fosters the development of internal diversity by the activities and functions that are specific to a city. It also fosters external diversity, as outsiders are attracted with their new ideas and diverse talents.

These internal and external dynamics of the city are underlain by a principal economic force: commerce and the market (Braudel 1967:385; Hannerz 1980:112). Indeed, the medieval city was a fertile terrain for the development of merchant capitalism, which, conversely, dramatically reshaped urban environments (Mumford 1964:328,522). Among the five domains within which city dwellers assume their numerous roles—home and family, provisioning, leisure, neighborhood relations, exchange—Hannerz (1980:136) postulates that provisioning is the basis for the exercise of all other roles. Consequently, an analysis of this role permits the most penetrating look into the urban phenomenon. This hypothesis has the merit of uniting individuals and the different roles they assume within the urban environment through the domain of provisioning. The individual has his place, or his niche, defined by his roles in urban ecosystems as can also be defined for animals in natural ecosystems. Also, this hypothesis has the advantage of defining an approach that can be applied in archaeology.

Through material vestiges, archaeology can address the vast domain of provisioning that includes the material resources needed to carry out urban roles. It can also identify the principal functions characterizing an urban environment and reconstitute the general outlines of an urban ecosystem. This model was applied to programmed research on the Hunt Block site in the Lower Town port district (L'Anglais 1994b:34-38, Auger and Moss 2002:138-141). By combining this ecosystemic framework with the wider approach of environmental archaeology—which reconstructs past landscapes defined as "the environment constructed by an urban population for its use" (Hannerz 1980:375; authors' translation)—it is believed that it will be possible to comprehend the urban ecosystem as a complete phenomenon and never lose sight of the individuals that actually live in the city. This approach will be used to draw an archaeological portrait of Quebec City, the colonial capital of New France during the French Regime.

The Archaeological Landscape of Quebec City during the French Regime

Quebec, a UNESCO World Heritage city, is alive and constantly changing. Most archaeological projects are associated with conservation or site development projects, or even more so, with urban development. Results of the individual interventions are not easily associated with a research design that can understand the city as a whole linked to dynamic processes in a regional or colonial context. Apart from several large-scale exceptions, archaeological projects have generally been characterized by numerous limited excavations undertaken in variable conditions and circumstances—Moss (1993) identified over 500 titles more than a decade ago—and it is difficult to develop a synthetic understanding of research results based on such a heterogeneous production.

Topography and geography offer the most advantageous starting point to study the landscape of the city (Figure 1). In a detailed analysis of these, Alain Painchaud (1993) identified eight factors that would have permitted human settlement at the location of the future city of Quebec. The narrowing of the St. Lawrence, the principal route of access into the heart of the continent, affords full control over the river, whereas the confluence with the St. Charles provides a secure harbor and a favorable environment for hunting and fishing. Insofar as topography is concerned, the relation between the St. Lawrence and the Cape Diamond promontory provides further advantages. The foreshore is narrow and shallow so that watercraft could easily land at the only habitable point on the bank, protected from predominant winter winds by the cliff above it. A ravine in the cliff front, today's *côte de la Montagne*, provided easy access to the plateau which provided an excellent view of the St. Lawrence and surrounding region. Several of these advantages were noted by Champlain, De Monts, and Gravé in 1603, and they certainly played a role in positioning the trading post on the point of land, Quebec Point, in 1608 (Champlain 1973 I:89-90,296).

Champlain's Trading Post, Montmagny's Town

The first French establishment at the foot of Cape Diamond would have a determining role on the form that the city would later take. The Lower Town would develop in its earliest phases around the *habitation*. Champlain quickly exploited the advantages offered by the promontory and constructed a wooden fort, the St. Louis fort, to protect the *habitation* at the foot of the cliff. Champlain planned on developing a city—to be named Ludovica—on the plains of the St. Charles River while reserving the Upper Town plateau for agriculture. Louis Hébert, New France's first settler, thus built his house on the plateau and began cultivating in 1617 (Rouleau 2003; Moss 2005; Simoneau 2008a). The Recollet friars constructed the St. Charles monastery on the south bank of the river of the same name in 1620 in what they believed would be the heart of the new city. They were followed five years later by the Jesuits who built a monastery on the opposing bank of the St. Charles (Morisset 1996:11-16). Both the Recollets and the Jesuits were to be proven wrong.

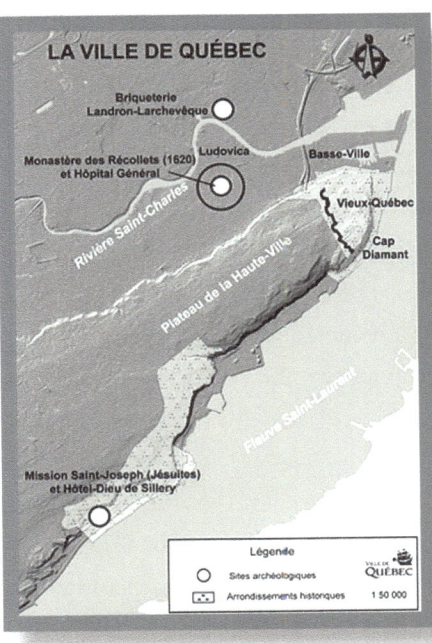

Figure 1.
The urban landscape of Quebec City and the archaeological sites outside the Old Town Historic District.

Following Champlain's death, New France's first official governor, Charles Huault de Montmagny, overturned his predecessor's urban project and implanted a radial town plan converging on the St. Louis fort on the Upper Town plateau. He replaced the frail wooden fortress by a masonry fort which also protected his official residence, the St. Louis château. The defensive works on the plateau would be the kernel of the Upper Town's development. In 1626, Champlain began a farm, the *Petite-Ferme*, to supply the new colony's livestock with hay. The *Petite-Ferme*, located 30 kilometers downstream, would never be more than an isolated outpost which, however, allowed it to retain its archaeological integrity (Guimont 1996).

Several nodes of settlement developed during the first decades of the colony and these would soon give rise to an urban network in the region. Seven kilometers upstream from Quebec Point in what would later become Sillery, the Jesuits founded the St. Joseph mission in 1637 with the intention of settling nomadic Native Americans. The *Hospitalières de Dieppe* joined them in 1640 and built the colony's first hospital, thus creating a hamlet that could have become a second urban center had they not withdrawn to Quebec in 1644 due to the threat of Iroquois attacks (Cloutier 2007). Several colonists settled in the Beauport seigneurie in 1634, and the Jesuits implanted a formally planned settlement in the Charlesbourg *Trait-Carré* in 1665. The following year, the Wendat Hurons, present in Quebec since 1650, settled in L'Ancienne-Lorette for a generation before moving to their present community, the village of Wendake.

This first phase of development of the urban landscape was largely determined by the topography of the site—the St. Lawrence River, Quebec Point, and Cape Diamond—

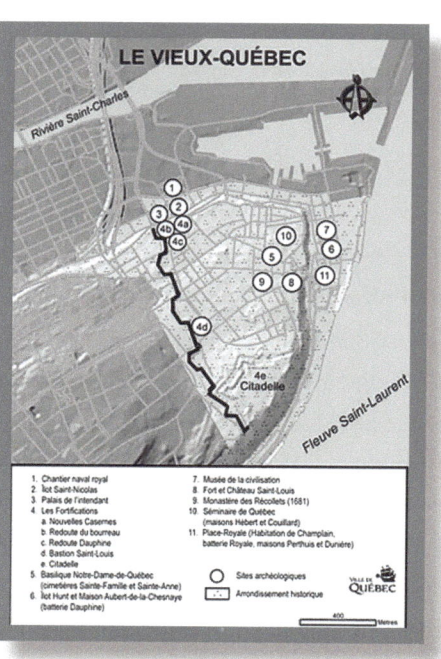

Figure 2.
The Old Town Historic District and the archaeological sites discussed in this chapter.

creating the Upper and Lower Towns early in its history. As the French were a minority to the Native American populations, some of whom with which they were in open warfare, the presence of fortifications was a determining aspect of the city from the very beginning. Commercial rivalry with New England and New Holland heightened the need for fortification works. Commercial activities necessitated port infrastructures (Figure 2). The merchant Lower Town, with the *place Royale* at the center of its grid-pattern layout, adapted the model of the medieval *bastide*, or walled town, throughout the 17th century. This model was often employed in colonial cities in the New World (Mumford 1964:420). The Lower Town was in sharp contrast to the Upper Town with its military, clerical and governmental institutions set in a Baroque radial town plan converging on the St. Louis fort and château (Mumford 1964:492; Chénier 1991:20-21). The menace of Iroquois attacks notwithstanding, the Upper Town fortifications did not completely enclose the city on the plateau until 1690 (Chénier 1991:27). Cannon batteries were erected along the shores of the St. Lawrence and the St. Charles in the Lower Town from the end of the 17th century onwards, and these strongly conditioned the nature of the port works of the French Regime.

Parks Canada archaeologists carried out a series of excavations on different sections of the Upper Town fortifications for more than 30 years. These projects were for the most part carried out during the maintenance and restoration of these vast works belonging to the Government of Canada (Beaudet and Élie 1993). Though the rhythm of these projects was determined by the requirements of architectural and engineering specialists, several major archaeological projects were accomplished: the Citadel, the St. Louis, Ursulines' and St. Jean bastions, the Dauphine Redoubt, the Palace Redoubt (or *redoute du Bourreau*), the Nouvelles casernes, the Palace Gate, and the St. Louis fort and château. These projects are of particular interest as they were executed with a coherent approach to maintain the same research design and methodology through time, thus allowing the systematic gathering of information on the fortifications (Beaudet and Élie 1993:27).

These projects achieved several goals such as determining the specific footprint of different constructions and analyzing the degree to which each system of earth, wood, or masonry respected 18th century military fortification theory. They also permitted the reconstruction of different elements such as a pepper box (*échaugette*) conceived to command both faces and the ditch on the point of a bastion (Beaudet and Élie 1993:29); the Palace Redoubt and its palisade, renamed the Hangman's Redoubt (*redoute du Bourreau*) around 1700 (Guimont and Savard 2000:4,10); and a temporary earthwork with its palisade and fraizing constructed in 1711 in the face of the threat of a new British invasion (L'Anglais 1999). Excavations on the St. Louis Fort and Château Site between 1985 and 1987 revealed remains of the southeast bastion built by Frontenac, four of six rectangular cannon platforms from the 1692 battery, as well as a trapezoidal platform from the 1740 battery (Renaud 1990:22-26). Further excavations were carried out inside the château by three campaigns from 2005 to 2007. Preliminary results indicate significant discoveries concerning this major institutional site that was the home of New France's governor during the French Regime.

Over 30 years of research on the Upper Town fortifications have provided abundant data on many poorly known aspects of French Regime lifeways in Quebec City. Insofar as the central theme of provisioning is concerned, a context from the St. Louis Bastion casemate, dating from 1750 to 1760, contained a rich deposit of bones, evidently culinary remains. The subsequent faunal analysis clearly indicated

that soldiers living in the casemate relied on a monotonous daily fare of beef or pork, and sometimes game and wildfowl such as hare and pigeon, or seafood such as cod and eel. This diet contrasted sharply with that of soldiers living in the 17th century Fort Chambly on the Richelieu River south of Montreal where substantial numbers of wild taxons (67 in all) complemented the same number of domestic taxons (Beaudet and Cloutier 1989).

Another significant contribution from the archaeology of the Upper Town fortifications came from the astonishing discovery of 52 burials during the reconstruction of the St. Louis Bastion (Gagnon 1990; Piédalue and Cybulski 1992). Stratigraphic analysis dated these burials between 1745 and 1753 when the fortifications were being rapidly completed following the declaration of the War of the Austrian Succession, which once again pitted France against England. Palaeoanthropological analysis identified an extraordinary group of individuals: 47 males as opposed to only four females and one youth. The men were of an average height of 173.3 cm, more than 8 cm taller than French soldiers from the fortress of Louisbourg at the same period. Archival research further suggested that these individuals were part of a group of 300 prisoners taken in New England and held in Quebec. The discovery of a bottle containing 5,000 pins and two knotted lengths of flax further reinforced this hypothesis as the practice of witches' bottles, meant to ward off evil spirits, was well known in England and New England at the time (Moussette 2006). This spell would have been needed given the numerous pathologies, such as scurvy and malnutrition, observed on the skeletal remains.

The First Lower Town

The Lower Town waterfront extended on two fronts: the first around Champlain's *habitation* on the St. Lawrence, and the second around the Intendant's Palace complex on the St. Charles. Each was vulnerable as neither was on raised land and both could be approached by boat. The Royal Battery, constructed on Quebec Point below *place Royale* in 1692, was the Lower Town's first work (Figure 3). The battery was excavated in 1972 by the Government of Quebec (Picard 1978) and rebuilt on its foundations. The first of several Dauphine Batteries was constructed to the north of the Royal Battery between 1707 and 1709. This battery constituted the embryo of the port's defensive works during the War of the Spanish Succession. Vestiges of the battery were uncovered by City of Quebec and Laval University archaeologists over a 15-year period (Harcart 1989; L'Anglais 1998; Leclerc 1998; Simoneau 2003, 2008b). A portion of the battery was integrated in the Auberge Saint-Antoine, a high-end boutique hotel, for display on the ground-floor level. The masonry wharves built parallel to the shore and capped by batteries resemble the royal ports built under Colbert on the shores of France between 1661 and 1685, particularly the ports of Brest, Lorient, and Rochefort on the Atlantic front.

These first works and the important infill that they required were the first expansion of the Lower Town's surface, which was too small for expanding commercial activity. There was considerable ambiguity about the maritime and defensive roles of the Dauphine Battery which, in time of peace, was a commercial wharf, but was rapidly transformed into a battery complete with embrasures with each approaching conflict (L'Anglais 1998:112). A second Dauphine Battery was constructed in front of the first with the beginning of the War of the Austrian Succession in 1745, extending the wharf surfaces further into deep water at the same time. Segments of this battery were robbed from the Hunt Block site by residents scavenging stone for new building in the ever-expanding Lower Town, but vestiges remained for 20th century archaeologists. Large portions of this battery, complete with mooring rings, remained intact immediately to the north and are now visible in the hall of the *Musée de la civilisation* (Laroche 1994:33). Further to the north, the stone wharves were completed by wooden constructions of "squared timbers piled one on the other and blocked by tie bars dove-tailed into the wharf-front" (Laroche 1994:34).

Figure 3.

The Old Town seen from the St. Lawrence River. The Lower Town is in the foreground, the Upper Town plateau is in the middle, while the St. Charles River valley extends to the northeast in the background. *Place-Royale* (1)—Champlain's *habitation*, the Royal Battery, the Perthuis and Dunière houses—the Hunt Block and the Aubert-de-la-Chesnaye site (2) and the *Musée de la civilisation* (3) are on the 17th century shoreline. The St. Louis fort (4) and the 1681 Recollets' Monastery (5) are on the top of the cliff. The Basilica (6)—the Ste. Anne and Ste. Famille cemeteries—and the Seminary (7)—the Hébert and Couillard houses—are also on the plateau. The Intendant's Palace and the Royal shipyards (8) are on the former banks of the St. Charles River. The Recollets's Monastery—located in the heart of the city of Ludovica (9)—are on the plain of the St. Charles, while the Landron-Larchevêque Brickyards (10) are on the first meander in the river.

The Second Lower Town

The second Lower Town, which grew up around the Intendant's Palace complex in the last quarter of the 17th century, was quite different from the first as it was on the estuary of the St. Charles River. Due to panic generated by

English attacks in the 1690s, a large palisaded compound was built around the Intendant's Palace and the St. Nicholas suburb. The St. Nicholas Redoubt protected the northwestern corner of this vast quadrant. This compound had little defensive value and it was never rebuilt. Part of the palisade closing the western flank of the site was nonetheless maintained and the redoubt appears on plans in the 18th century as it protected the entrance to the St. Charles River.

The Intendant's Palace Site has been the most intensively researched part of the of the second Lower Town through a series of campaigns from 1982 to 1990 (Moussette 1994), and from 2000 to 2007 (Dionne 2001; Duchaine 2001; Lapointe 2001; Eid 2003; Gilbert 2003; Alberton 2005; Herzog 2005) by Laval University and the City of Quebec (Simoneau 2008c). Five major phases of occupation have been identified for the period before 1763: 1) Native American; 2) early Euro-American; 3) Talon's brewery (1668–1675); 4) the first Intendant's Palace (1684–1713); and 5) the second Intendant's Palace and King's Storehouses (1716–1760).

Only several objects, including a stone projectile point and a polished-stone adze, have been found in the earliest levels of a late-Woodland Amerindian occupation. The earliest levels associated with a European presence indicate woodworking activities, possibly part of shipbuilding on the St. Charles estuary in the 1660s. Abundant wood chips and sawdust and pieces of worked wood were found in the 2007 season. Vestiges associated with the intendant Talon's brewery are more imposing and easy to identify. The exact outline of the building and numerous components of the brewing process have been excavated. These include the malt house floor and cistern; draining tiles; two vents and a drain; the drying tower for transforming sprouted barley into malt; and heating ovens for boiling wort in copper kettles. This imposing industrial building influenced the urban fabric of the suburb. Indeed, the intendant De Meulles chose this abandoned building for his quarters in 1684. The excavation of levels associated with this period revealed

modifications to the brewery to house the intendant and his suite: dungeons for the King's prisoners and four cellars used as storerooms for the King's goods, as witnessed by the huge quantity of gun parts, trade knife blades, religious medallions, and barrel parts found in them.

These objects afford abundant information about the intendant's role and influence as far away as the Mississippi, but they also inform us about France's commercial activities and the provisioning of its troops. In light of the continuing threat of English invasion, the western ramparts of the city were extended to the Lower Town by connecting the Palace and St. Nicolas redoubts. These works also influenced the urban landscape and important vestiges have been discovered on the Intendant's Palace Site: the base of a massive masonry wall connecting the Upper and Lower Town works; the masonry foundations of another building, probably another redoubt protecting a gate to the intendant's compound; and a series of posts forming the palisade that continued on to the St. Roch Redoubt.

A fire destroyed the Intendant's Palace in 1713, leaving only the foundations and the masonry walls to the west. This led to a reorganization of the whole complex with a new palace, larger and more monumental than the first, being constructed on the northern side of the compound, facing the Upper Town rather than the St. Charles. A new King's Storehouse was built on the ruins of the first palace. Excavations carried out since 2000 have uncovered those vaults destroyed in the 18th century and the latrines that were in service from 1720 to 1760. The rich material recovered from these latrines will supply abundant information on the material culture of this period once analysis has been completed.

Excavation of the four basement rooms of the new storehouses also produced examples of merchandise and goods stored in them: gun parts for repairing the troops' weapons and trade goods such as folding knives, decorated gun parts, religious medallions, and pewter rings. Exploratory excavations were undertaken on the site of another storehouse set inside an adjacent potash factory built by the intendant Jean Talon (Lapointe 2001). Other elements from this period include a significant element of the urban landscape, a section of the paved road that linked the two poles of secular power in New France, the Intendant's Palace and the Governor's residence in the St. Louis Château. This was the only paved road surface in New France. They also include vestiges of the coach house and components of a drainage system and a pool in the adjacent poultry yard. A basin and canal allowing boats and merchandise access to the storehouses were set on the northern limit of the first Intendant's Palace towards the St. Charles River in the latter part of the 17th century. Several excavations have been designed to locate this significant component of the compound, but results are as yet inconclusive.

Nascent Industries

The St. Charles was a central part of the early town for other reasons. A shipyard was constructed immediately downriver from the Intendant's compound at the St. Nicolas Block. The first shipyard was active from 1666 to 1702 (Brisson 1983:45), but to date, archaeological research has mostly addressed the second shipyard in operation from 1732 to 1739, encountering vestiges of a mole, wharf structures, and a slipway (Loewen and Cloutier 2003:23). Analysis of these elements permits their interpretation in the context of changing approaches to shipbuilding in the 18th century, indicating that the Quebec yards were "at the cutting edge of scientific debates then underway in the maritime world" (Loewen and Cloutier 2003:39). Wood waste and tools from the St. Nicolas Block further speak of shipbuilding, while coarse earthenware kiln waste indicates the presence of Jean Aumier, a potter who was active from 1673 to 1703 (Tremblay and Véronneau 1988). Recent compositional analysis of the kiln waste confirms that the coarse earthenware was made from local clay deposits (Monette 2005). Research has also been conducted on the

site of the Landron-Larchevêque brickworks, in operation from 1688 to 1765 further upstream on the left bank of the St. Charles River (Goyette 2004).

While the Intendant's Palace compound strongly ensconces the institutional nature of the area, the presence of Talon's brewery, the potash works, the shipyards, and the pottery highlight the industrial character of the Lower Town. The presence of the Landron-Larchevêque brickyards upriver further demonstrates that the St. Charles River valley was the industrial core of the colony at the end of the 17th century. Indeed, tanneries, new breweries, and numerous other potteries would be constructed along this river throughout the 18th and 19th centuries.

The City: Provisioning and Lifeways

Vestiges of defensive works and port infrastructures mark the physical limits of the urban entity, but research must also address the contents and the specific functions of this space. The first Lower Town is generally defined by the presence of merchants and the Upper Town by institutions, but what can archaeology contribute to this portrait?

Urban development and architectural reconstruction projects have been the motor of research undertaken in the first Lower Town, particularly in the *Place-Royale* sector. Results from numerous interventions carried out over more than four decades by archaeologists with diverse training, experience, and methodologies have been difficult to exploit to their full potential. This is as much true of the Hunt Block Site, excavated by Laval University and the City of Quebec, as of the *Musée de la Civilisation* Site, from which material has yet to be analyzed 20 years after excavation. It is true as well of the *Place-Royale* project, excavated by the Quebec Culture and Communications Department, and from which historical and archaeological data have yet to be analyzed with a model adapted for urban archaeology, though material culture studies from this latter project have come to be a very significant contribution to historical archaeology in general (Auger and Moss 2002).

Despite the absence of a synthesis of the archaeology of the first Lower Town, *Place-Royale* remains the principal point of interest due to the intensity of activity in the heart of the commercial city as shown by the historical synthesis of the site (Côté 2000). Also, the presence of merchants meant that commercial activities were concentrated in this sector. An analysis of provisioning activities, when combined with an approach to the urban landscape, permits a better understanding of the dynamic forces present in the urban context. Several partial syntheses have been produced on sites from within the *Place-Royale* sector: Rouleau et al. (1998a) on the Aubert-de-la-Chesnaye House, Niellon and Moussette (1985) on Champlain's *Habitation*, and L'Anglais (1994a) on the Dunière and Perthuis houses. The latter will be considered more closely as L'Anglais's analysis, based on the concept of "household," casts light on the process of provisioning, the central notion of this study.

One specific context from this site—the rich latrines from the second quarter of the 18th century—is of particular interest here. The 772 ceramic and glass artifacts excavated from the latrines indicate the importance that the merchant Perthuis—who lived in the house from 1741 to 1750—attributed to expressing his high social status in the colony (L'Anglais 1994a:331-337). Many of the artifacts showed no wear marks so they were probably associated with Perthuis's commercial ventures, thus bringing us to the heart of the provisioning process. These objects were largely from France, but many came from England, Spain, Italy, Holland, Bohemia, Germany, or China. Local provisioning was restricted to foodstuffs as seen from osteological analysis indicating that Perthuis raised pigs, chickens, and turkeys in his courtyard. This analysis also indicated that mammals represented the principal source of meat. The ratio of domestic to wild taxons—7/17 or 0.41—further suggest that commercial or sport hunting and fishing were being carried out beyond the limits of the

city. This portrait is very different from that of the early days of the trading post where salted meats imported from France were predominant.

As a corollary of the analysis of lifeways and provisioning, L'Anglais's research design addresses urban hygiene through practices associated with refuse disposal. This is a central aspect of how urban ecosystems function. Céline Cloutier (1996a:18-24) further examined this question through the analysis of latrines from the Aubert-de-la-Chesnaye Site dating from 1680 to 1702. These latrines were built with stone vaults and an opening permitting their cleaning and evacuation into the St. Lawrence. They were replaced with dry pits, then by water closets in the 1820s, following the arrival of British merchants after the Conquest.

The Upper Town

The Upper Town, at first agricultural before becoming institutional, with its sparse buildings and numerous gardens in contrast with the dense urban fabric of the Lower Town, can be examined from the same perspective (Figure 4). During the 17th century, before the construction of the fortification systems, the Upper Town plateau could have been mistaken for a suburb of the commercial district along the waterfront. The plateau was home to major institutional, military, and government actors in the colony: the St. Louis fort and château (1635), the Hôtel-Dieu hospital (1642), the Ursulines' Convent (1642), the Jesuits' College (1650), the Seminary (1666–1675), the Recollets' Monastery (1681), the Cathedral—later a basilica—(1684–1697), and the Bishop's Palace (1692).

The Seminary complex, built from 1666 onwards, contains some of the only traces of the first phase of Quebec City as planned by Champlain (Cloutier 1996b; Moss 2005; Simoneau 2008a). Champlain's city, Ludovica, would have been built in the St. Charles River valley, whereas the plateau would have been the site of fields and pastures, as witnessed by the colony's first colonists, Louis Hébert and his son-in-law Guillaume Couillard, starting their Sault-au-Matelot farm between 1617 and 1621 on the future site of the Upper Town's Seminary. Little—even the exact location—was known about the colony's first farms as the geographic information noted in the first decades of the 17th century is no longer visible in the urban landscape. A series of excavations in the 1990s offered a new perspective on this sparsely documented period. The Couillard house was partially excavated in 1992 in the Seminary courtyard while Hébert's house was discovered in the Seminary

parking lot in 1994; both offered some of the first concrete information on the layout of the nascent city. Personal objects found in Couillard's house, including numerous

Figure 4.
A series of archaeological sites ring the Château Frontenac hotel in the Upper Town: vestiges of the St. Louis fort and château under excavation in the fall of 2007 are at the top of the cliff (1); the 1681 Recollets' Monastery is under the Anglican cathedral (2); the Ste. Anne and Ste. Famille cemeteries are on either side of the Basilica (3); the Seminary complex, with its numerous wings, is built on Louis Hébert's farm in 1666 (4).

Figure 5.
The Dauphine Redoubt (1) and the *Nouvelles casernes* (2), two components of the Upper Town fortifications, overlook the Intendant's Palace (3). The Royal Shipyards, formerly on the banks of the St. Charles River, lie under the *place de la Gare* (4). Work is underway for the construction of the *pavillon Jean-Talon* above the vestiges of the first Intendant's Palace.

trade beads, suggest that Hébert and Couillard participated in the black-market fur trade despite a legal ban. This is in sharp contradiction to the classic image of New France's first farmers presented in 19th-century historiography!

The St. Louis fort and château would become the heart of the city's layout once Montmagny turned his back on Champlain's urban project, abandoning Ludovica and building his city on the Upper Town plateau. Results of research on this site were discussed earlier.

Excavation of the Recollets' Monastery Site—the monastery built in 1681 on the site of today's Holy Trinity Anglican Cathedral—uncovered vestiges of the east wing of the General Hospital built in 1689 and contexts associated with the Recollets' hospice from 1681 onwards (Rouleau 1998b). The most innovative data supplied by this project concerns the monastery's gardens. Archaeologists identified egg shells and fish bones used as fertilizer in soil horizons associated with the garden (Rouleau et al. 1998b:84-85). Seed remains indicated the presence of garden vegetables and of medicinal and ornamental plants, allowing a beginning to reconstructing the floral landscape (Fortin 1998:265). Archaeological research has also offered insight into the foodways of the sites' occupants: garden vegetables, cultivated and wild fruit, and meats coming from domesticated mammals, with beef coming first on the list followed to a lesser degree by game. Seven domestic taxons were identified compared to 14 wild taxons, for a ratio of 0.50, which indicates a more varied diet than that of soldiers billeted in the St. Louis Bastion casemate.

The consecrated grounds of cemeteries are an important part of the urban landscape and are important repositories for memories. Analysis of human remains from several cemeteries has given us direct information on the population itself. To date, two cemeteries from the French Regime have been analyzed. Both—Ste. Anne (1691–1844) and Ste. Famille (1657–1841)—were adjacent to Notre-Dame-de-Québec Cathedral, and results offer an interesting portrait of 17th and 18th century city dwellers. Firstly, and insofar as provisioning of drinking water is concerned, excavations indicated that underground springs filtered through the cemeteries' soils before being drawn from the Seminary's kitchen well some dozens of meters downhill. These excavations provide a graphic example of how urban hygiene could be sorely wanting, even in the heart of the young colony (Simoneau 2008a).

Palaeoanthropologist Robert Larocque's (2000) analysis has given us a sobering image of a once-optimistic evaluation of New France's inhabitants' state of health. Serious

pathological conditions were identified: a high degree of morbidity at weaning resulted from developmental problems of the fetus; rickets within the female population caused obstetrical accidents and stillbirths; poor teeth and joints were signs of premature aging from the age of 40 onwards. Larocque (2000:124) cautions that more data are needed to confirm these interpretations, but important avenues of research have been identified.

The Landscape of a French Port

After the precariousness of the trading post at the foot of the plateau cliff, the fortifications facing the St. Lawrence on one side, or the hinterland on the other, imprint a lasting mark on the landscape of Quebec City from the 1690s onwards. The fortifications can be seen as the principal

Figure 6.
Vestiges of Charles Aubert de la Chesnaye's wharves and the Dauphine Battery are visible during excavations on the Hunt Block in 2001. These vestiges have been integrated into the architecture of the Auberge Saint-Antoine.

elements conferring the status of "city" on the colonial town. As demonstrated by the historian Alain Guillerm (1985), fortifications are the physical expression of France's dominion over land and sea. As such, Quebec's landscape can be compared to that of French metropolitan seaports from the same period, particularly of those developed under Colbert to consolidate the Royal navy. The physical signs of this hegemony are the vestiges, often lost and forgotten, of curtain walls, bastions, or batteries that are revealed by archaeological interventions (Figure 6). Even more so, the vestiges of the waterfront fortifications, the King's batteries erected over private wharves, and the Royal shipyards building oceangoing vessels and small craft for inland commerce, are all representative of the predominant relationship of the city to its principal waterway, the St. Lawrence River.

A full understanding of the importance of the St. Lawrence as the main route into the interior of the continent allows a more complete understanding of the importance of Quebec City as a symbol of the permanence of French power in North America, a role going well beyond its mere significance as a defensive location. Both the Lower—the first and second—and Upper Towns, each with its distinctive characteristics, developed as gradually evolving expressions of this fundamental postulate.

Quebec and the Colonial Context of New France

Having completed the synthesis of the city of Quebec's archaeological landscape, the city now will be examined in the wider colonial context of New France. The phenomenon of urbanization is a process going beyond a single urban center and it must be studied as a series of "functionally and socially interdependent agglomerations seen both internally and in terms of hierarchically articulated relations (an urban network)" (Castells 1972:32; authors' translation). In other words, the creation of one city implies the creation of others. This is particularly true in a colonial context where the creation of a series of specialized centers—such as staging posts on commercial networks, outposts, service centers for agricultural communities, or resource extraction towns—can be seen following the development of an initial central urban place.

In Canada, this process began in Quebec City, moving up the St. Lawrence, the "sovereign axis of the colony" in the words of the historian Jacques Mathieu (2001:46). As a part of this movement, Jesuit missionaries were present in Huronia in 1632. Quebec City would soon be accompanied by two other strategic posts, Three Rivers at the mouth of the St. Maurice River in 1634, and Montreal at the confluence of the St. Lawrence and Ottawa rivers in 1642. The three urban centers formed the core of the settlement of the St. Lawrence valley. Montreal was incontestably more important as an urban center than Three Rivers. Its archaeological potential has been largely exploited, which is unfortunately not the case for Three Rivers.

Topographic differences are the first contrast that can be noted when comparing Montreal and Quebec. In Montreal, the *coteau Saint-Louis*, a hillside sloping gently up from the mouth of the slow-moving St. Pierre River, is very dissimilar from Quebec with the St. Lawrence and its seven-meter high tides and the narrow terrace below the escarped face of Cape Diamond. The differentiation between an upper and a lower town is barely perceptible in Montreal. A sole town plan, a grid pattern developed inside of the 1680s wooden palisade that has been partially excavated by archaeologists, overlays the hillside (Lelièvre and Cloutier 2001:23-24; Groupe de recherche en histoire du Québec and SACL 2003:137-140). The town plan, implemented by the Sulpician friar Dollier de Casson in 1672, is that of a walled town (Marsan 1974:111-116)—a *bastide*—as was that of Quebec's Lower Town during its initial days as a forward trading post.

Montreal's fortifications were constructed during a period of open warfare with the Iroquois, and they served as a refuge for the settlers from the surrounding countryside. The wooden palisade was replaced by masonry walls in 1717, but these were never used to defend the city from attack (Marsan 1974:102; Recherches Arkhis 2003:83-84). The defensive value of these works has been open for debate, and some have said that their primary purpose was to keep Native Americans, come to Montreal to trade furs, out of the city (Recherches Arkhis 2003:8-9; Marsan 1974:103). This is, at the least, indicative that Montreal assumed an important commercial role at the end of the 17th century, eclipsing its importance as a defensive refuge or an advance post.

Trading between French and Native Americans took place on the riverbank at the confluence of the St. Lawrence and St. Pierre. Several archaeological sites bear witness to these exchanges, as is the case of the *pointe à Blondeau*, which also housed the sheds used for the storage of freight canoes used on the route to the North-West (Ethnoscop 2003). Montreal, with its fort set back from the river on a gentle slope, had a very different appearance from Quebec with its institutional Upper Town and its Lower Town with wharves and batteries.

Montreal would remain an essential link in the fur trade for all of the French Regime. Furs would arrive from the interior of the continent by way of a series of relays and trading posts, and they would then be forwarded on to Quebec where they would in turn be put on seagoing vessels and shipped to France. Results from research on the house of two wealthy Montreal fur merchants, Charles Le Moyne and Jacques Le Ber, illustrates Montreal's particular situation (Ethnoscop 2003). Material excavated from the site includes many items of trade with Native Americans—Micmac pipes, glass beads, tinkling cones, flakes of European flint, a catlinite pipe coming from far-off Minnesota—as well as high-status goods meant to express the merchants' importance—finely decorated tin-glazed earthenware, high quality table glass, and the bones of a very rare peacock. Once again, the omnipresence of material culture remains of relations with Native Americans

differentiates archaeological contexts in Montreal from those of Quebec.

According to the historian W.J. Eccles (1976), this manner of occupying the territory was specific to Canada and contrasted sharply with that of Americans. In his celebrated study of the frontier in the history of the United States, Frederick Jackson Turner portrays the westward expansion of Euro-Americans as an unfolding wave, with the frontier being the boundary between them and Native Americans: "In this advance, the frontier is the outer edge of the wave—the meeting point between savagery and civilization" (Turner 1965:3), with civilization being for him Euro-American society while savagery was reserved for Native Americans. As seen by Turner, this advancing frontier, pushed by a large population of settlers seeking "free land," resulted in the conquest of Native American populations, decimated by disease and lacking the technical means of the settlers, reduced to minorities no longer able to resist.

For Canada, French expansion into the west was of a very different nature from that of their British neighbors to the south (Eccles 1976:9). The metaphor of an unfurling wave used by Turner cannot be applied here. In the latter case, a solid base of permanent establishments along the St. Lawrence served as staging grounds for a series of trading posts that, all in all, had a minor impact on Native American populations. The French and their descendants, the *Canadiens*, quartered in advance posts, were always a small minority amongst their Native American hosts who they had to treat with deference, in contrast to British and American colonists. As trade was the principal reason for French presence, the back-and-forth movement between the St. Lawrence valley urban centers and the advance trading posts was constant. This maintained a certain degree of "civilization" for those participating in the exchanges, thus maintaining French culture in far-flung centers. Furthermore, as the main urban centers were all on the banks of the St. Lawrence, the constant transit of travelers, *coureurs de bois*, Native Americans, merchants, missionaries, and soldiers brought the frontier to the doorstep of homes in the heart of the colony.

This is far different from the model proposed by Turner where settlers progressively lose contact with the older establishments of the Atlantic coast as they develop a new and specifically American mentality in their western movement. In Canada, the forging of a new identity happened in the very heart of the colony along the St. Lawrence River in constant contact with the Native American world and the vast expanses of the interior of the continent. The role of Quebec in the colonial context, a fortified city poised at the narrowing of the St. Lawrence on the limit of oceangoing navigation during the French Regime, was that of the Atlantic port for the frontier of French expansion into the New World.

ACKNOWLEDGMENTS

We would like to thank André Nault for his plans, Pierre Lahoud for his aerial photographs, and Diane Bussières of Bussières Communications for computer graphics.

REFERENCES

ALBERTON, LORENZO

2005   *Rapport d'intervention, le Palais de l'intendant: opération 40 (2002).* Cahiers d'archéologie du CELAT, no 17. CELAT, Ville de Québec and Ministère de la Culture et des Communications du Québec, Quebec, Quebec, Canada.

AUGER, RÉGINALD, AND WILLIAM MOSS

2002   The Archaeology of Physical and Social Transformation: High Times, Low Tides and Tourist Floods on Quebec City's Waterfront. In *The Archaeology of Urban Landscapes, Explorations in Slumland,* Alan Mayne and Tim Murray (editors), pp. 132-144. Cambridge University Press, Cambridge, England.

AVIGNON, MATHIEU D'

2006   Champlain et les historiens francophones du Québec: les figures du père et la mythe de la fondation. Ph.D. Thesis. Université Laval, Quebec, Quebec, Canada.

BEAUDET, PIERRE, AND CÉLINE CLOUTIER

1989   *Les témoins archéologiques du fort Chambly.* Environnement Canada, Lieux et parcs historiques nationaux, Service des parcs, Ottawa, Ontario, Canada.

BEAUDET, PIERRE, AND MONIQUE ÉLIE

1993   Les fortifications de Québec. *Mémoires vives* 5:25-32.

BRAUDEL, FERNAND

1967   *Civilisation matérielle et capitalisme (XVe-XVIIIe siècle), Vol. 1.* Armand Colin, Paris, France.

1979   Le temps du monde. In *Fernand Braudel, Civilisation matérielle, économie et capitalisme XVe-XVIIIe siècle, Vol. 3.* Armand Collin, Paris, France.

1985   *La dynamique du capitalisme. Champs 192.* Flammarion, Paris, France.

1997   Expansion européenne et capitalisme (1450–1650). In *Les écrits de Fernand Braudel, Vol. 2: les ambitions de l'histoire.* Rosalyne de Ayala et Paule Braudel (editors), pp. 299-345. Éditions du Fallois, Paris, France.

BRISSON, RÉAL

1983   *La charpenterie navale à Québec sous le Régime français.* Institut québécois de recherche sur la culture, Quebec, Quebec, Canada.

CASTELLS, MANUEL

1972   *La question urbaine.* François Maspero, Paris, France.

CHAMPLAIN, SAMUEL DE

1973   *Œuvres de Samuel de Champlain,* Vol. 1. Éditions du Jour, Montreal, Quebec, Canada.

CHÉNIER, RÉMI

1991   *Québec ville coloniale française en Amérique: 1660–1690.* Environnement Canada, Ottawa, Ontario, Canada.

CLERMONT, NORMAN, CLAUDE CHAPDELAINE, AND JACQUES GUIMONT

1992   *L'occupation historique et préhistorique de Place Royale.* Collection Patrimoine. Dossier 76. Ministère des Affaires culturelles du Québec, Quebec, Quebec, Canada.

CLOUTIER, CÉLINE

1996a   Hygiène privée, transferts culturels et mécanisation: le cas des latrines du site Aubert de la Chesnaye à Québec. In *L'eau, l'hygiène et les infrastructures,* pp. 17-24. Groupe PGV, Montreal, Quebec, Canada.

1996b   Deuxième partie. Des siècles piétinés: aperçu de la collection archéologique du Séminaire de Québec. In *Recherches archéologiques dans la cour des petits du Séminaire de Québec (CeEt-32),* pp. 201-261. Ville de Québec and Ministère de la Culture et des Communications du Québec, Quebec, Quebec, Canada.

2007   *La mission des Jésuites et l'établissement du premier Hôtel-Dieu à Sillery: évaluation du potentiel archéologique.* Ville de Québec and Ministère de la Culture et des Communications du Québec, Quebec, Quebec, Canada.

CÔTÉ, RENÉE

2000   *Place Royale: Quatre siècles d'histoire.* Fides, Montreal, Quebec, Canada.

DIONNE, MARIE-MICHELLE

2001   *À la recherche des vestiges du nouveau palais de l'intendant enfouis sous la rue Des Prairies: l'opération 33, intervention archéologique 2000.* Cahiers d'archéologie du CELAT, no 9. CELAT, Ville de Québec and Ministère de la Culture et des Communications du Québec, Quebec, Quebec, Canada.

DUCHAINE, DÉSIRÉE-EMMANUELLE

2001   *De 1693 à aujourd'hui, secteur de la rue Vallière à l'ouest du palais de l'intendant: l'opération 34, intervention archéologique 2000.* Cahiers d'archéologie du CELAT, no 9. CELAT, Ville de Québec and Ministère de la Culture et des Communications du Québec, Quebec, Quebec, Canada.

ECCLES, W. J.

1976   *The Canadian Frontier, 1534–1760.* University of New Mexico Press. Albuquerque.

EID, PATRICK

2003   *Le secteur de la rue Vallière à l'ouest du palais de l'intendant: CeEt-30, opération 37.* Cahiers d'archéologie du CELAT, no 15. CELAT, Ville de Québec and Ministère de la Culture et des Communications du Québec, Quebec, Quebec, Canada.

ETHNOSCOP

2003   *Présence amérindienne et occupations marchandes: Fouille archéologique au site Lemoyne-Leber (BjFj-49), 1999.* Collection patrimoine archéologique de Montréal 19. Ville de Montréal, Montreal, Quebec, Canada.

FORTIN, CATHERINE

1998   *Troisième partie: Analyse paléo-ethnobotanique du site du monastère des récollets.* In *L'archéologie du monastère des récollets à Québec,* pp. 241-285. Cahiers d'archéologie du CELAT, no 4. CELAT, Ville de Québec and Ministère de la Culture et des Communications du Québec, Quebec, Quebec, Canada.

FOX, EDWARD WHITING

1973   *L'autre France: L'histoire en perspective géographique.* Flammarion, Paris, France.

GAGNON, CLAIRE

1990   Énigme dans les remparts de Québec. *Québec Science* 28(7):24-28.

GILBERT, LOUIS

2003   *Le site du deuxième palais de l'intendant à Québec (CeEt-30), opération 3b: intervention archéologique 2001 sur la rue Des Prairies.* Cahiers d'archéologie du CELAT, no 15. CELAT, Ville de Québec and Ministère de la Culture et des Communications du Québec, Quebec, Quebec, Canada.

GOYETTE, MANON

2004   Découverte d'une briqueterie du XVIIe et XVIIIe siècles à Québec: la briqueterie Landron-Larchevêque. *Archéologiques* 17:45-61.

GROUPE DE RECHERCHE EN HISTOIRE DU QUÉBEC AND SACL

2003   *La chapelle Notre-Dame-du-Bon-Secours.* Collection Patrimoine archéologique de Montréal 22. Ville de Montréal, Montreal, Quebec, Canada.

GUILLERM, ALAIN

1985   *La pierre et le vent: Fortifications et marine en Occident.* Arthaud, Paris, France.

GUIMONT, JACQUES

1996   *La Petite-Ferme du cap Tourmente. De la ferme de Champlain aux grandes volées d'oies.* Septentrion, Sillery, Quebec, Canada.

GUIMONT, JACQUES, AND MARIO SAVARD

2000   *Autour des Nouvelles casernes.* Éditions Continuité, Quebec, Quebec, Canada.

HANNERZ, ULF

1980   *Explorer la ville.* Éditions de Minuit, Paris, France.

HARCART, LE GROUPE

1989   *Les îlots Bell et Hunt: inventaire archéologique.* Ville de Québec, Service de l'urbanisme, Quebec, Quebec, Canada.

HERZOG, ANJA

2005   *Rapport de la XIIe campagne de fouilles: l'îlot des palais de l'intendant, CeEt-30, opération 38 (été 2002).* Cahiers d'archéologie du CELAT, no 17. CELAT, Ville de Québec and Ministère de la Culture et des Communications du Québec, Quebec, Quebec, Canada.

L'ANGLAIS, PAUL-GASTON

1994a   *Les modes de vie à Québec et à Louisbourg au milieu du XVIIIe siècle à partir de collections archéologiques.* Collection Dossiers, no 86. Ministère de la Culture et des Communications du Québec, Quebec, Quebec, Canada.

1994b   *La recherche archéologique en milieu urbain: d'une archéologie dans la ville vers une archéologie de la ville.* Les Cahiers du CELAT, hors série 6. CELAT, Ville de Québec and Ministère de la Culture et des Communications du Québec, Quebec, Quebec, Canada.

1998   *Le site de l'îlot Hunt: rapport de la deuxième campagne de fouilles (1992).* Cahiers d'archéologie du CELAT, no 2. CELAT, Ville de Québec and Ministère de la Culture et des Communications du Québec, Quebec, Quebec, Canada.

1999   Une redoute temporaire en terre et en bois construite en 1711: observations sur les pieux découverts à la redoute Dauphine en 1972. *Archéologiques* 13:20-32.

LAPOINTE, RICHARD

2001   *Le bâtiment de la potasse de Québec: d'une industrie du XVIIe siècle aux industries du XXe siècle.* Cahiers d'archéologie du CELAT, no 9. CELAT, Ville de Québec and Ministère de la Culture et des Communications du Québec, Quebec, Quebec, Canada.

LAROCHE, DANIEL
1994   L'archéologie des installations portuaires à Québec. *Mémoires Vives* 6-7:31-35.

LAROCQUE, ROBERT
2000   *La naissance et la mort à Québec autrefois: les restes humains des cimetières de la basilique Notre-Dame-de-Québec.* Cahiers d'archéologie du CELAT, no 5. CELAT, Ville de Québec and Ministère de la Culture et des Communications du Québec, Quebec, Quebec, Canada.

LECLERC, MYRIAM
1998   *Appropriation de l'espace et urbanisation d'un site de la basse ville de Québec.* Cahiers d'archéologie du CELAT no 1. CELAT, Ville de Québec and Ministère de la Culture et des Communications du Québec, Quebec, Quebec, Canada.

LELIÈVRE, FRANCINE, AND CÉLINE CLOUTIER
2001   *Louis-Hector de Callière: Homme de guerre, homme de paix.* Presses Inter Universitaires, Cap-Rouge, Quebec, Canada.

LOEWEN, BRAD, AND CÉLINE CLOUTIER
2003   Le chantier naval royal à Québec et le savoir maritime au XVIIIe siècle. *Archéologiques* hors série 1:23-42.

MARSAN, JEAN-CLAUDE
1974   *Montréal en évolution: historique du développement de l'architecture et de l'environnement montréalais.* Fides, Montreal, Quebec, Canada.

MATHIEU, JACQUES
2001   *La Nouvelle-France: Les Français en Amérique du Nord, XVIe-XVIIIe siècle.* Les Presses de l'Université Laval, Quebec, Quebec, Canada.

MONETTE, YVES
2005   Éclairages nouveaux sur les céramiques locales et leurs provenances : le cas du Québec méridional, c1680–1890. Ph.D. thesis. Université Laval, Quebec, Quebec, Canada.

MORISSET, LUCIE
1996   *Patrimoine du quartier Saint-Roch. La mémoire du paysage. Histoire de la forme urbaine.* Ville de Québec and Ministère de la Culture et des Communications du Québec, Quebec, Quebec, Canada.

MOSS, WILLIAM
1993   Cent vingt-cinq ans de découvertes. *Mémoires vives* 15:4-24.

2005   Quebec City, Canada. In *Unlocking the Past; Celebrating Historical Archaeology in North America.* Lu Ann De Cunzo and John Jameson (editors), pp. 82-88. The Society for Historical Archaeology and University Press of Florida, Gainesville.

MOUSSETTE, MARCEL
1994   *Le site du Palais de l'intendant à Québec: genèse et structuration d'un lieu urbain.* Septentrion, Sillery, Quebec, Canada.

2006   L'épingle et son double en Nouvelle-France. *Les Cahiers des Dix* 60:103-128.

MUMFORD, LEWIS
1964   *La cité à travers l'histoire.* Éditions du Seuil, Paris, France.

NIELLON, FRANÇOISE, AND MARCEL
  MOUSSETTE
1985 *L'Habitation de Champlain.* Collection Dossiers,
       no 58. Ministère des Affaires culturelles du
       Québec, Quebec, Quebec, Canada.

ODUM, EUGÈNE P.
1976 *Écologie.* Éditions HRW, Montreal, Quebec,
       Canada.

PAINCHAUD, ALAIN
1993 *Paléogéographie la Pointe de Québec (Place-
       Royale).* Collection Dossiers, no 68. Ministère de
       la Culture du Québec, Quebec, Quebec, Canada.

PICARD, FRANÇOIS
1978 *La batterie royale, de la fin du XVIIe siècle à la fin
       du XXe siècle.* Collection Civilisation du Québec,
       no 23. Ministère des Affaires culturelles, Quebec,
       Quebec, Canada.

PIÉDALUE, GISÈLE, AND JÉRÔME CYBULSKI
1992 Les sépultures des fortifications de Québec: une
       histoire oubliée. *Mémoires Vives* 3:4-12.

RECHERCHES ARKHIS
2003 *Les fortifications de Montréal: Recherche
       archéologique au Champ-de-Mars (BjFj-21,
       1990–1991).* Collection Patrimoine archéologique
       de Montréal 6. Ville de Montréal, Montreal,
       Quebec, Canada.

RENAUD, ROXANE
1990 Par la bouche de mes canons. In *Les dessous de la
       terrasse à Québec.* Pierre Beaudet (director), pp.
       21-29. Septentrion, Sillery, Quebec, Canada.

ROULEAU, SERGE
2003 *Recherches archéologiques, fouilles de la maison
       Couillard et surveillance, cour des Petits du
       Séminaire de Québec, CeEt-32, 2002.* Ville

de Québec and Ministère de la Culture et des
       Communications du Québec, Quebec, Quebec,
       Canada.

ROULEAU, SERGE, CÉLINE CLOUTIER, C. FORTIN,
AND L'OSTÉOTHÈQUE DE MONTRÉAL INC.
1998a *L'archéologie de la maison Aubert-de-la-
       Chesnaye à Québec.* Cahiers d'archéologie
       du CELAT, no 3. CELAT, Ville de Québec and
       Ministère de la Culture et des Communications du
       Québec, Quebec, Quebec, Canada.

ROULEAU, SERGE, DOMINIQUE LALANDE, C.
FORTIN, AND L'OSTÉOTHÈQUE DE MONTRÉAL
INC.
1998b *L'archéologie du monastère des Récollets à
       Québec (CeEt-621).* Ville de Québec and Ministère
       de la Culture et des Communications du Québec,
       Quebec, Quebec, Canada.

SIMONEAU, DANIEL
1995 *Rapport d'inventaire archéologique: Les jardins
       du Séminaire de Québec.* Ville de Québec and
       Ministère de la Culture et des Communications
       du Québec, Quebec, Canada.

1996 Première partie: Rapport de fouilles archéologiques
       dans la cour des petits du Séminaire de Québec.
       In *Recherches archéologiques dans la cour des
       petits du Séminaire de Québec (CeEt-32).* William
       Moss (director), pp. 1-200. Ville de Québec and
       Ministère de la Culture et des Communications du
       Québec, Quebec, Quebec, Canada.

2003 *Rapport d'intervention archéologique à l'îlot
       Hunt, 2001.* Ville de Québec and Ministère de
       la Culture et des Communications du Québec,
       Quebec, Quebec, Canada.

2008a   *Le Séminaire de Québec: 140 ans de recherches archéologiques.* Cahiers d'archéologie du CELAT, no 22. CELAT, Ville de Québec and Ministère de la Culture et des Communications du Québec, Quebec, Quebec, Canada.

2008b   *L'îlot Hunt: vingt ans de recherches archéologiques.* Cahiers d'archéologie du CELAT, no 23. CELAT, Ville de Québec and Ministère de la Culture et des Communications du Québec, Quebec, Quebec, Canada.

2008c   *Rapport d'étape du projet de fouilles archéologiques sur le site du Palais de l'Intendant.* Réalisées par la Ville de Québec: saisons, 2006–2007. Ville de Québec and Ministère de la Culture et des Communications du Québec, Quebec, Quebec, Canada.

TREMBLAY, KATHERINE, AND FRANÇOIS VÉRONNEAU
1988   *Rapport de fouilles et de surveillance archéologiques: l'îlot Saint-Nicolas, phase 3.* Ville de Québec, Service de l'urbanisme, Quebec, Quebec, Canada.

TRUDEL, MARCEL
1963   *Histoire de la Nouvelle-France I: Les vaines tentatives, 1524–1605.* Fides, Montreal, Quebec, Canada.

TURNER, FREDERICK JACKSON
1965   *The Frontier in American History.* Holt, Rinehart and Winston, New York, NY.

WALLERSTEIN, IMMANUEL
1984   Le mercantilisme et la consolidation de l'économie européenne. *Le système du monde du XVe siècle à nos jours,* Vol. 2. Flammarion, Paris, France.

Marcel Moussette
Département d'histoire
Université Laval
1030, Avenue des Sciences-Humaines
Québec (Québec)
Canada G1V 0A6

William Moss
Ville de Québec
295 Boulevard Charest Est
Québec (Québec)
Canada G1K 3G8

CARMEL SCHRIRE

THE MATERIAL WORLD OF THE ENGLISH AT JAMESTOWN, VIRGINIA AND THE DUTCH AT THE CAPE OF GOOD HOPE

ABSTRACT

Links are explored between the first English settlement at Jamestown and the first Dutch settlement at the Cape of Good Hope. Jamestown was part of the colonial Atlantic world whereas the Cape lay in the European-Asian network of a major trading company. The material remains in a series of Cape archaeological sites are presented and interpreted in their geographic, economic, social, and ideological contexts.

Thirteen years after the first settlers landed at Jamestown Island, an English fleet bound for Asia anchored at the southernmost tip of Africa. Europeans had been calling in at the Cape since 1488 when Portuguese mariners christened it *Cabo de Tormentoso* (Cape of Storms), a name that they later changed to the more salubrious *Cabo de Bonne Esperanza* (Cape of Good Hope) to bless their singular victory in opening up the seaway to India (Raven-Hart 1967:2). On this particular occasion, the English were certain that a neighboring Dutch fleet planned to make a plantation here (Raven-Hart 1967:106). Their captain rose immediately to the challenge and took possession of the bay and its great mountain by raising a cairn, which he named in honor of his king, "King James His Mount"

(Raven-Hart 1967:107). At that instant the Cape became one of many Jamestowns that marked the path of English colonial expansion in the early 17th century, joining a scatter of outposts underwritten by royalty in Spain and Portugal or by private shareholders in England, France, and the Netherlands, and setting the stage for the global economy that we have today.

Whatever the English had in mind at the Cape that day in 1620, they did not behave like the crew who anchored off the Virginian Jamestown in 1607. Instead of solidifying their claim with a fort and a garrison, they sailed away leaving the Cape to whomever had a mind to do the job properly. Thirty-two years later, in 1652, after a good look at their financial situation, the Dutch planted a fort on the beach. The venture was funded and run by the Dutch East India Company, or VOC (*Verenigde Oostindische Compagnie*), which had been operating in the East for 50 years. Like Jamestown in Virginia, the Cape settlement was a business venture, but unlike it, the Cape was specifically settled to provision the shipping between the homeports of the Netherlands and the Company's foreign trade in Asia. Unlike the Virginia Company, the VOC was large and very powerful. It had its own army, minted its own coinage, and dispensed justice under its own courts. It might have been nominally responsible to the States General, but its first duty was to its investors and the last thing it wanted to hear were the discontented opinions of the indigenous owners or the European settlers at the Cape. This single-mindedness paid off for a long and profitable time until the Company went bankrupt in 1795, after which the Cape became a British colony.

The historical archaeology of the VOC settlement of the Cape has another Virginia connection. In 1984 Jim Deetz visited the University of Cape Town. Until then, historical sites at the Cape had been recognized but excavations had been limited to rescue operations. Public disinterest in colonial relics contrasted markedly with the enthusiastic concern with prehistoric archaeology (Deacon and Deacon 1999), to say nothing of the relish with which the rulers

Figure 1.
View of the Castle of Good Hope showing the settlement, Table Bay, and the plan of the "Fort" or Castle. N. de Fer, Paris, 1705. (S. Schrire collection).

of the apartheid state memorialized their origin myths, reenacting events like the 1652 landing at the Cape, the 1688 arrival of the French Huguenots, the frontier wars against the Bantu kingdoms, and the Boer War against each other. Deetz wasted no time on the niceties of ideology. Instead, he encouraged scholars to set their sights on creating an archaeological record of colonial expansion to expose parallels and insights between colonial settlements here and in the New World. The outcome was a number of archaeological projects based on competitive and contractual funding that generated a picture of the Cape settlement in a world perspective. This paper describes some aspects of this work, specifically the finds from three Cape sites, namely the Castle of Good Hope in central Cape

Town; Oudepost I, a VOC outpost 120 km to the north; and the colonial farm of Elsenburg located about 50 km east of the Castle (Schrire 2010).

The original VOC fort on the beach was dismantled between 1665 and 1674 and cannibalized to help construct the Castle of Good Hope, a massive stone structure that still stands in the center of the city of Cape Town today (Figure 1). The design followed the basic defensive principles of the Old Dutch System (*Oudnederlands stelsel*), with a central courtyard surrounded by a main wall (*hooftwal*) with five bastions, ringed in turn by an underwall (*onderwal*), surrounded by a moat and counter slope. The interpretation of its archaeological residues rests on four observations. First, the Castle was not built on sterile ground but on a surface littered with prehistoric residues of Stone Age people. Second, although it was first occupied in 1674, reconstruction and restoration continue to this day, generating a constant production of secondary deposits. Third, the Castle has always had a water problem: it stood on the shores of Table Bay at the confluence of mountain streams and high tides, and infilling was constantly done to keep it dry. Finally, although the Castle was designed for defense, it was never actually attacked. Instead, it functioned as a small, walled town, housing men and women, rulers, soldiers, slaves, free blacks, and a wide variety of craftsmen. It was a hub, where people lived on the leavings of the past, generating new residues that were redisposed as fills to raise storage rooms, halls, and kitchens out of the rising damp.

Archaeological research began at the Castle in the mid-1970s in concert with major restorations. The largest project ran from 1988 to 1992 and involved excavations by the Archaeology Contracts Office at the University of Cape Town under the direction of Professor Martin Hall. Key sites excavated at this time include the Old Granary (F2), the infilled Moat (M90), and the floor of a vaulted room called Donkergat ("Dark Hole") (DKG). The oldest archaeological deposit found to date comes from the lowest levels of the Old Granary (pre-1685 to mid-18th century). Later deposits come from the infilled Moat and date from ca. 1690–1740 (Yates et al. c.1994-1995). The Donkergat residues are undated and contain patent kitchen debris in the form of burnt, cooked, and butchered bones. The lower levels of the Old Granary (F2) were interpreted originally as primary deposits of underclass slaves, who behaved like their counterparts in Virginia by digging pits as hidey-holes to stow the expensive porcelain stolen from their masters in acts of subaltern resistance (Hall 1992:389-390). Recent analysis of the "pits" and their associated residues suggests that this interpretation is unfounded. The rubble, charcoal, and broken bones, chewed over by dogs, have no apparent links to slaves, but instead are part of a secondary fill generated elsewhere and dumped here probably as part of an overall strategy to keep the space dry. Similarly, the infilled Moat, which was originally seen as a secondary dump for ceramics, bones, rubble, and charcoal that emanated from the Castle, now seems to have served also as a depository for bones, hides, and offal from a butchery or shambles on the adjacent beach (Heinrich 2010).

The second site, Oudepost I, was excavated between 1984 and 1995. It was a VOC frontier outpost located about 120 km north of the Cape on the lagoon of Saldanha Bay, the largest inlet on the African coast. Manned by a small garrison from 1669 to 1732, its chief purpose was to provision passing ships with water, fresh vegetables, and meat. The station was supplied officially from the Cape settlement and nearby VOC farms, and informally from passing ships and by hunting and fishing. The archaeological residues include primary deposits in the sand around the small stone-walled lodge and fort, and secondary dumps in the rock pools and muds of the intertidal zone (Schrire 1995) (Figure 2).

Figure 2.
View of the Excavation of the Company Lodge at Oudepost I, Cape, looking east across the Langebaan lagoon, Saldanha Bay. Scale in 20 cm increments. (C. Schrire 1986).

Finally, the old farm x lies about 50 km east of Cape Town on the slopes of the Hottentot's Holland Mountains. The archaeological collections were excavated by the University of Cape Town Contracts Office in 1993, and were interpreted as a fill lying under the kitchen of the main house. Analysis of ceramics and pipe stems were used to date the collection to the second quarter of the 18th century (Hart and Halkett 1993) (Figure 3).

Figure 3.
View of the farm Elsenburg, Cape, showing sluice, slave bell, and outbuildings. (C. Schrire 2005).

Analysis of these collections provides a broad view of the material culture of the VOC Cape. The ceramics are dominated by a variety of Asian wares including Chinese and Japanese Export Wares and Coarse Porcelain Ware. Persian fritware is rare, as are stonewares that include Martevan jars and red Yi-xing teapots, and earthenwares. The richest and best-analyzed collection comes from the Castle Moat where Chinese wares predominate, forming over 90% of the total collection, followed by Japanese wares (3-6%), and a smattering of the rest. These collections may be dated according to their archaeological context, and by using archival records and shipwreck cargoes. For instance, the first official shipment of Persian fritware appears in the VOC records of 1666 (Volker 1954:115; Klose 1992–1993:71). Where the majority of Asian wares are concerned, shipwreck cargoes confirm their late-17th- to early-18th-century age (Christie's Amsterdam 1992; Klose 1999–2000; Chien 2002; Werz 2004). Tightly dated patterns confirm these estimates, as in the cases of Moat tea wares with the "Rotterdam Riots" pattern (1690) (Howard and Ayers 1978:60, No. 15), and a bowl with the "eight horses of Emperor Mu Wang" (1660–1670), from Oudepost I (Schrire et al. 1993:29).

The Asian collections at all three sites contrast strongly with the wider range and higher quality seen in archaeological finds of the same period in the Netherlands, which relate to social differences of class and wealth between places like metropolitan Amsterdam as opposed to the peripheral, impoverished Cape settlement. This interpretation is confirmed by the presence of the enameled wares. Around 1730 these wares were more expensive than blue and white, and their very low frequency at the Cape points to a small market for such expensive goods there. Although Chinese Export wares cost more than the others, the overall quality found at Cape sites is nothing near as high as that found in Holland or, for that matter, in the kitchen debris of a wealthy Cape burgher at the mid-18th-century site of Elsenburg. Such contradictory evidence as exists, is more apparent than real. For example, an occasional quality piece, like the bowl with the eight horses of the Emperor

Mu Wang, or a *famille verte* cup found at Oudepost, probably says nothing about the wealth of a resident at the outpost, because it was probably dumped off a visiting ship. Likewise, although Japanese monogrammed wares are now costly collectors' items, those found in the Moat and Oudepost I were not luxury goods, but rather, ceramics specifically requisitioned for use on VOC settlements and outposts in much the same way as monogrammed wares are supplied to institutions, hotels, and cruise ships today (Figure 4). Some Japanese wares found at the Cape were relatively expensive, but their small persistence in all levels of the sites speaks less to wealth than to the fact that the Cape lay within the ambit of this particular inter-Asian trade, which went on until 1757 (Jörg 2003).

Figure 4.
Monogrammed VOC Japanese plate,
Castle of Good Hope (C. Schrire 2006).

Turning to coarse earthenwares, they include tin- and lead-glazed wares. Tin-glazed earthenwares were all imported and can be classified mainly as "faience." They form a small part of the collections and are more common in the older contexts such as the Old Granary (F2) and Oudepost I than in the later Moat deposits. Lead-glazed vessels include imported fine-grained, pale-bodied,

European wares like Nederrhein and Bergen op Zoom, as well as locally made, coarse-grained red-bodied wares. No clear internal site sequences are visible although local wares definitely predominate throughout the later Moat deposits. These variations may be due in part to the nature of the sites: Oudepost was a recipient of imported goods off passing ships, whereas refuse generated by the Castle garrison, including the big vessels in which their food was cooked, often ended up in the open Moat ditch. Where style and function are concerned, the VOC imported European potters to make local Cape wares, and the typologically European forms they produced may be interpreted as a Dutch colonial South African version of colonoware. Finally, Cape collections contrast with their European counterparts in their patent lack of dairy vessels, as opposed to their high proportion of stewing pots to accommodate the syncretic Cape-Asian cuisine, with its heavy diet of stewed meat flavored with Oriental spices (Jordan and Schrire 2002) (Figure 5).

European stonewares at the Cape include mainly vessels for beverage transport, storage, and drinking. The collections do not show the diversity seen in European collections, lacking, as they do, mustard pots, salt pots, chamber pots, and decorated drinking vessels. Instead, Rhenish jugs predominate in all three sites, with numerous large, plain ones in the Castle Moat reflecting the same principle of garrison provisioning as was noted in the presence of large, locally made, coarse earthenwares. Finally, a small component of Westerwald ware is present in all collections, especially at Oudepost I, where they probably represent gifts from passing ships. Most have 18th-century schematic, incised, cobalt-filled and stamped, and knibiswood mold-pressed decorations, in contrast to the applied relief designs of earlier times (Gaimster and Hildyard 1997; Jordan 2010).

Glasswares were all imported and the Cape collections are dominated by bottles and table wares. Typologically similar collections are found in all the sites, though there is a striking absence of large bottle fragments at Oudepost due to persistent depredations of bottle collectors there. Onion-mallet and case bottles occur in roughly equal proportions, and they all have heavy wear on the bases that reflects repeated reuse over time. The bulbous onion bottles were mainly made in Belgium for wine, beer, oil, and vinegar and became known as "Dutch" from their trade in the distant colonies, including Suriname and Guyana

Figure 5.
Cape manufactured kookpot (M90 CEW 102), Moat, Castle of Good Hope, Cape (C. Schrire 2007).

(Van den Bossche 2001:119). Square case bottles with flat bases and short necks evolved from common utility bottles to a more tapered form that carried gin into the 18th century. Here they resemble Dutch/German/Belgian bottles of the 17th to 18th centuries (Van den Bossche 2001:131-133). In addition, huge *karbassen*, or carboys, used in taverns to store wine, appear in the Castle sites, and small pharmaceutical bottles are found in the Moat and at Oudepost I. Table wares include goblets, roemers, and beakers engraved with Chinoserie designs that echo the associated porcelains. The only fragment of façon de Venise comes from the uppermost level of the Old Granary (F2).

Metal artifacts from the outpost of Oudepost I include the iron, lead, and copper wares like hammers, picks, shovels, trowels, nails, chisels, daggers, knives, barrel staves, and objects of trade. Evidence of firearms comes from a large collection of European gunflints, as well as from lead rolls, shot, and bullet molds (Figure 6). The VOC imported copper in rings and sheets from Japan for trade with the natives, and the archaeological remains include sheet copper neatly cut and chiseled into triangles, rectangles, and circles. Other trade goods, including glass beads, point

to trading relations. Finally, items of personal decoration are consistent with the predominantly male occupants of the Castle and its outpost, and include buckles and buttons that reveal the presence of both low ranking soldiers of the "unqualified" class and higher-ranking men (White 2010).

Where faunal remains are concerned, the collections reveal a combination of farming and hunting consistent with historical records of early settlement at the Cape. The indigenous Khoekhoen were hunters and pastoralists whose herds were a major factor in the decision of the VOC to settle the Cape as a ships' provisioning post. A vibrant cattle trade developed that quickly overwhelmed the authority of the indigenes. Colonial collections register this process in the increasing presence of native cows, hybrid sheep, imported pigs, horses, and fowls, as opposed to a steady decrease in game. The huge faunal collection from the Moat is dominated by hybrid sheep that were mostly slaughtered at prime age. Both sheep and cattle show signs of primary butchery, with the meatier parts having been removed at a nearby shambles in order to provision the garrison and/or passing ships. In contrast to this, the mixture of weathered, trampled, and burned bones in the Old Granary (F2) confirms that the deposit is

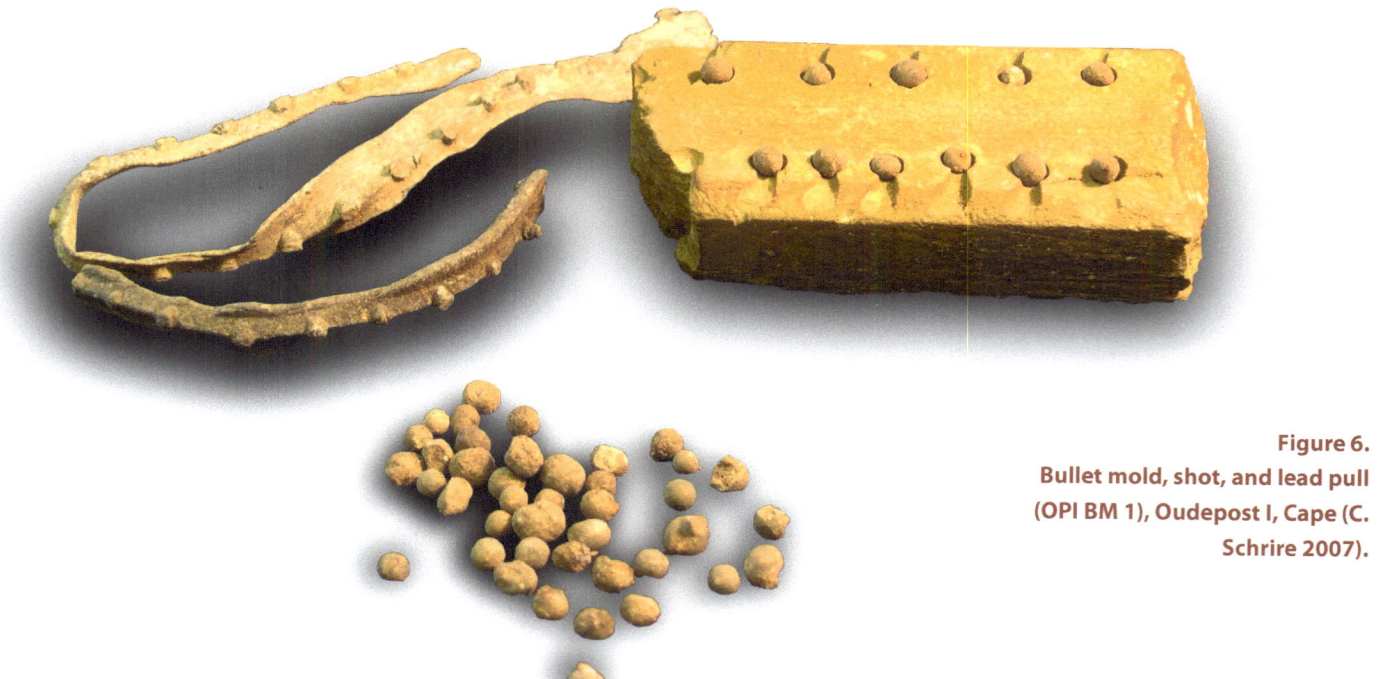

**Figure 6.
Bullet mold, shot, and lead pull
(OPI BM 1), Oudepost I, Cape (C.
Schrire 2007).**

a secondary fill of mixed origin. Sheep predominate in the kitchen debris at another Castle locale of DKG, where there is evidence that beef and pork were also eaten (Heinrich 2010). The ships' provisioning station at Oudepost I has two different faunal components: refuse scattered around the settlement is dominated by wild fauna, sheep, and very few cattle, and probably accumulated in the course of daily life, whereas refuse dumped in the sea has more cattle and was probably generated in periods of ships' provisioning. The management of VOC herds is revealed in an analysis of sheep remains from the kitchen dump at the farm of Elsenburg. Here, old female sheep predominate, suggesting that younger ones were sent to market, to reappear in the butchered and burned residues at places like the Castle and Oudepost I (Cruz-Uribe and Schrire 1991; Schrire 1995:106-110; Heinrich 2010).

Comparisons between the Cape and Virginia reveals some interesting variations in the network of far-flung sites in the old colonial world. By the time these Cape collections were deposited in moats, pits, fills, and sandy ruins, the Jamestown settlement had grown, though the original fort had been abandoned for decades. The VOC Cape was never a jewel in the crown of the Company; it was a poor and small outpost that was regarded as a stepping-stone to more favored posts in the East. Most of the people there worked under Company orders, and even those who set themselves up as private farmers or tradesmen operated under the constraints of VOC monopolies, taxes, and regulations. Material evidence reveals local differences in wealth and status. Asian porcelain is rare at Jamestown, and the occasional sherd suggests a wealthy owner able to cover the markup incurred in the long trip from China via Europe to Virginia, whereas similar porcelain at the Cape was affordable by rich and poor alike, and simply reflects VOC preference for cheaper, more durable Asian wares shipped in from their entrepot in Batavia, Java. Majolicas are the most common European wares at Jamestown (Kelso 2006:177) but are practically unknown at the Cape where a smattering of faience occurs mainly in earlier deposits. This may be because the Jamestown settlement is older than

the Cape, and that Nederrhein wares were more popular in the Netherlands markets when the Cape was flourishing. Both settlements depended on Europe for bottles and for stoneware flasks, importing plain Rhenish jugs—heirs to a long European potting tradition—that were valued for their immediate contents and then reused, again and again, for whatever liquid might be around.

Settlers at the Cape and Jamestown both traded in beads, copper, and all the paraphernalia of narcotic exchange encoded in bottles and tobacco pipes. Metallurgy and assaying were practiced at both locales, but more complicated distillation ceramics appear in Virginia. Cape crucibles never are encrusted with glass as they are at Jamestown, nor, in contrast to Jamestown, is there any evidence that the VOC ever used indigenous pots as crucibles (Kelso 2006:181-184). This may be because Cape Khoekhoen pots were friable and badly fired, as opposed to the more durable Powhatan vessels in Virginia, or it may be that the need to assess the commercial potential of the New World was a more urgent priority at Jamestown than at the Cape, where the economic priority was ships' provisioning.

Moving to organic residues, although hard times were commonplace in the early years of settlement, unlike Jamestown there is no "Starving Time" recorded at the Cape. The most striking thing about the Cape collections is the way they denote an ideological shift in European identity, switching from dairymen, "cheese-heads," and eaters of "white meat" to become highly carnivorous pastoralists. The Dutch started modifying the native sheep as soon as they landed at the Cape by importing breeds from Persia and Europe to produce a meatier hybrid (Mentzel 1944:210). They did not get around to hybridizing Cape cattle until 130 years later, and even then the official and systematic importation of cattle only took root under British rule in the early 19th century (Thom 1942:103-105). In short, the VOC settlement at the Cape ate mutton and used native cows for draft and, to a lesser extent, for meat rather than for milk, encoding these practices in their coarse earthenwares that were not used for butter and cheese, but for stewing meat.

The question is why did they abandon their North European traditional identity as dairy farmers with such apparent alacrity? Historians, veterinarians, and agronomists are quick to rationalize the situation by noting that Cape cattle are poor milkers and good draft animals. A colonial dairy industry was unlikely to have been productive because there was no money to be made exporting butter, sheep were easier to manage, and hybrid sheep produced better meat than sinewy draft oxen. There is a paradox here though, because for all their commitment to a European identity as soldiers, servants, or dignitaries of the great Dutch East India Company, the VOC stock farmers at the Cape ended up looking more like the very people they displaced and were supposed to despise. Economically speaking, the Cape settlers resembled indigenous, transhumant Khoekhoen pastoralists rather than their relatives back home (Thom 1942:111-113; Heinrich 2010).

This transformation is just one aspect of colonial change. In Jamestown, former soldiers became farmers and some poor settlers harvested enough tobacco to become rich. At the Cape the poor folk of Europe turned to farming and trading, and many flourished as farmers on lands taken from the native people. In the early years of Cape settlement, ships' provisioning remained its highest priority and imports far outweighed exports. The native Powhatan of Virginia and Khoekhoen at the Cape became incorporated into new worlds as foreign pathogens depleted the people and guns wiped the land clear of game (Figure 6). The Cape Khoekhoen knew nothing of Jamestown, though they did not like Virginia tobacco and preferred black Brazilian weed (Schrire 1995:157). And everyone forgot that there was once a monument there called "King James His Mount."

ACKNOWLEDGMENTS

I wish to thank Bill Kelso, Bly Straube, and the APVA team for their collegiality over the past 15 years. I also am grateful to the Center of Human Evolution, Department of Anthropology, Rutgers; to The State University of New Jersey, for financial support; and to Stacey Jordan, Carolyn White, and Adam Heinrich for sharing their work on the Cape collections. Above all, I thank the members of the Department of Archaeology at the University of Cape Town, especially my friend Jane Klose, for years of help and support.

REFERENCES

CHIEN, NGUYEN DINH

2002   *The Ca Mau Shipwreck, 1723–1725.* The National Museum of Vietnamese History, Hanoi.

CHRISTIE'S AMSTERDAM

1992   *The Vung Tau Cargo. Chinese Export Porcelain.* Sale catalog, April 1992.

CRUZ-URIBE, KATHRYN, AND CARMEL SCHRIRE

1991   Analysis of Faunal Remains from Oudepost I, an Early Outpost of the Dutch East India Company, Cape Province. *South African Archaeological Bulletin* 46:92-106.

DEACON, HILARY J., AND JANETTE DEACON

1999   *Human Beginnings in South Africa: Uncovering the Secrets of the Stone Age.* D. Phillips, Cape Town, South Africa.

GAIMSTER, DAVID R. M., AND ROBIN J. C. HILDYARD

1997   *German Stoneware 1200–1900: Archaeology and Cultural History: Containing a Guide to the Collections of the British Museum, Victoria and Albert Museum, and the Museum of London.* British Museum Press, London.

HALL, MARTIN

1992   Small Things and the Mobile, Conflictual Fusion of Power, Fear, and Desire. In *The Art and Mystery of Historical Archaeology, Essays in Honor of James Deetz,* Anne Elizabeth Yensch and Mary C. Beaudry, editors, pp. 373-399. CRC Press, Boca Raton, FL.

HART, TIM, AND DAVID HALKETT

1993   Archaeological Investigation of the Elsenburg Herenhuis. Archaeological Contracts Office, Department of Archaeology, University of Cape Town, South Africa.

HEINRICH, ADAM ROBERT

2010   Faunal Analysis and the Development of the VOC Meat Industry at the Cape. In *The Material Culture of the VOC at the Cape of Good Hope 1652–1800,* Carmel Schrire, editor. Left Coast Press Inc., Walnut Creek, CA.

HOWARD, DAVID SANCTUARY, AND JOHN AYERS

1978   *China for the West: Chinese Porcelain & Other Decorative Arts for Export Illustrated from the Mottahedeh Collection.* Sotheby Parke Bernet, London, England.

JORDAN, STACEY CHRISTINE

2010   Coarse Earthenware Collections from VOC Sites at the Cape. In *The Material Culture of the VOC at the Cape of Good Hope 1652–1800,* Carmel Schrire, editor. Left Coast Press Inc., Walnut Creek, CA.

JCRDAN, STACEY CHRISTINE, AND CARMEL SCHRIRE

2002   Material Culture and the Roots of Colonial Society at the South African Cape of Good Hope. In *The Archaeology of Colonialism. Issues and Debates,* Claire L. Lyons and John K. Papadopolous, editors, pp. 241-272. Getty Research Institute, Los Angeles, CA.

JÖRG, CHRISTIAAN J. A.

2003   *Fine and Curious: Japanese Export Porcelain in Dutch Collections.* Hotei, Amsterdam, The Netherlands.

KELSO, WILLIAM M.

2006   *Jamestown: The Buried Truth.* University of Virginia Press, Charlottesville.

KLOSE, JANE

1992-1993

Excavated Oriental Ceramics from the Cape of Good Hope 1630–1830. *Transactions of the Oriental Ceramic Society* 57:69-81.

1999-2000

Oriental Ceramics Retrieved from Three Dutch East India Company Ships Wrecked off the Coast of Southern Africa: the *Oosterland* (1697), *Bennebroek* (1713) and *Brederode* (1785). *Transactions of the Oriental Ceramic Society* 64:63-81.

MENTZEL, OTTO F.

1944 *A Complete and Authentic Geographical and Topographical Description of the Famous and (All Things Considered) Remarkable African Cape of Good Hope (1787): Part Three.* H. J. Mandelbrote, revision and editor, G.V. Marais, J. Hoge, translators. Van Riebeeck Society 25, Cape Town, South Africa.

RAVEN-HART, MAJOR ROWLAND

1967 *Before Van Riebeeck: Callers at South Africa from 1488 to 1652.* C. Struik, Cape Town, South Africa.

SCHRIRE, CARMEL

1995 *Digging through Darkness: Chronicles of an Archaeologist.* University Press of Virginia, Charlottesville, VA.

SCHRIRE, CARMEL (EDITOR)

2010 *The Material Culture of the VOC at the Cape of Good Hope 1652–1800.* Left Coast Press Inc., Walnut Creek, CA.

SCHRIRE, CARMEL, KATHERINE CRUZ-URIBE, AND JANE KLOSE

1993 The Site History of the Historic Site at Oudepost I, Cape. In *Historical Archaeology in the Western Cape*, Martin Hall and Ann Markell, editors, pp. 21-32. *South African Archaeological Bulletin Goodwin Series*, No. 7.

THOM, HENDRIK BERNARDUS (EDITOR)

1942 *Willem Stephanus van Ryneveld se Aanmerkingen over de Verbetering van het Vee aan de Kaap de Goede Hoop 1804.* Van Riebeeck Society, No. 23, Cape Town, South Africa.

VAN DEN BOSSCHE, WILLY

2001 *Antique Glass Bottles: Their History and Evolution (1500–1850). A Comprehensive, Illustrated Guide, with a World-Wide Bibliography of Glass Bottles.* Antique Collectors' Club, Woodbridge, Suffolk, England.

VOLKER, T.

1954 *Porcelain and the Dutch East India Company.* E. J. Brill, Leiden, The Netherlands.

WERZ, BRUNO E. J. S.

2004 'Een bedroefd, en beclaaglijck ongeval': De Wrakken van de VOC-Schepen *Oosterland* en *Waddinxveen* (1697) in de Tafelbaai. Walburg Pers, Zutphen, The Netherlands.

WHITE, CAROLYN L.

2009 Analysis of Objects of Personal Adornment from VOC Sites at the Cape. In *The Material Culture of the VOC at the Cape of Good Hope 1652–1800*, Carmel Schrire, editor. Left Coast Press Inc., Walnut Creek, CA.

YATES, ROYDEN, STEPHAN WOODBOURNE, AND
MARTIN HALL
1994-1995
       The Chronology of Colonial Settlement at the Cape
of Good Hope: Clay Tobacco Pipes. Department
of Archaeology, University of Cape Town, South
Africa.

Carmel Schrire
Department of Anthropology
Ruth Adams Building, 3rd floor
School of Arts and Sciences
Rutgers, The State University of New Jersey
131 George Street
New Brunswick, NJ 08901-1414

www.ingramcontent.com/pod-product-compliance
Lightning Source LLC
Chambersburg PA
CBHW041428120626
46547CB00002B/134